SUNDAY TELEGRAPH

# 101 WAYS OF INVESTING & SAVING MONEY

# SUNDAY TELEGRAPH

# 101 WAYS OF INVESTING & SAVING MONEY

## ALEX MURRAY

Published by Telegraph Publications
135 Fleet Street, London EC4P 4BL

First published September 1983
© *Sunday Telegraph* 1983
Second edition, updated, March 1984
Third edition, updated, April 1985
ISBN 0 86367 051 2

Printed in Great Britain by
Cox and Wyman, Reading
Typeset by Sunset Phototype Ltd, Barnet

# Preface

The up-turn in the economy which began four years ago has been sustained. Businessmen are showing greater confidence now, despite the volatility of sterling, and consumers are still spending money in the shops. One of the main factors in the British recovery has been the considerable improvement in personal wealth over the last few years. This has been reflected in the rise of the stock market, the strength of house prices and the fall in inflation.

This book, first published in 1983, resulted from many inquiries by *Sunday Telegraph* readers who were unable to find elsewhere a comprehensive guide to the wide range of savings and investment opportunities available. For the first time, we assembled details of every conceivable form of investment, from saving money with a bank or building society to buying wine, old cars, horses and, of course, stocks and shares. There is much more besides – in fact we have listed 101 ways of investing money productively.

In this latest edition, we have taken account of various tax changes from the 1985 Budget and of alterations in other markets and investments since last year. The book was written by Alex Murray, our Deputy City Editor, with Philip Beresford, helped by Sylvia Howe. It is not intended to be a complete reference book on each indivdual area, but an easily understandable guide to the various options, noting the possible pitfalls and offering tips and useful addresses. It also outlines taxation implications of investment. For more details on this see another successful *Sunday Telegraph* publication, *101 Ways of Saving Tax*. I hope our readers become even more prosperous with this edition.

**Ian Watson, City Editor, March 1985**

# Contents

## III National Savings

## IV Stocks and shares

## X USEFUL ADDRESSES

# I
# Introduction

**What are the advantages of saving money, as opposed to**   **1**
**investing it or spending it?**

By whatever route it comes to you, money is an asset
worth preserving, unless you have so much of it that
this does not matter – in which case you are one of a
lucky and very small percentage of the population. If
you are a salaried employee, you may be able to
accumulate savings every month to spend at your leisure, either as a lump sum or in a system of regular
payments. If you inherit money, it may come in the
form of property or money – cash or investments. If
you win the pools, make a killing on the stock market
or are made redundant, you may suddenly find you
have a large sum of money to take care of. Or if you
are self-employed, your business may be earning you
enough money to warrant careful planning of your
financial opportunities, rather than simply letting the
business take care of itself.

Whatever your circumstances, it is vital – though it
is perhaps obvious to say so – that you decide for what
purpose you need to plan ahead, if at all. If you have
made all your plans already, then you may be looking
only to safeguard your present standard of living. You
may be prepared to consider some of the more
speculative investments which may lose you all you
put into them, or may double or triple your money.
On the other hand, if you have a family or other

dependents, and only a small amount to spare, you will need to make sure that your money is invested wisely.

Spending money on the needs of daily life is something that most people think of in different terms from investment and savings – and, of course, buying food, groceries, household equipment, and so on, sees very little return, except in the standard of living which you have chosen. But even here, it is worth thinking about the longer term. Who would have thought, after all, that the Dinky toys which so many parents bought their children in the 1950s and 1960s would have turned out to be a very promising investment (when properly preserved)? At the same time, the car you choose may, when looked after carefully, turn out to have some financial benefit to you rather than simply being a means of transport.

It goes without saying that if you decide to spend a windfall on the good life – drink, gambling and other expensive pleasures – then you have thrown caution to the winds, and can expect to have little left but memories. But if you would like to keep your money in some more longer-lasting, tangible form, then investing it or saving is preferable. Of course, there are moments when spending money, rather than investing or saving, makes financial sense in itself. For example, in the period of near-30 per cent inflation in the mid-1970s average household goods were worth buying and storing in some quantity, because one knew that they would almost certainly be more expensive later. But such periods are difficult to predict. Anyway, this is really a form of investment akin to buying Chinese porcelain or good wine.

Perhaps the key distinction between spending money and investing it is time. Investing implies that whatever you have bought will be sold later, and some form of gain will be realised, while spending is mostly short-term. The distinction becomes somewhat blurred when you look at things like wine and furniture, which you may keep for many years and enjoy yourself. The key to investment is to buy something for the purpose of seeing your money grow, or to buy something cheaply now which will be more expensive in a few years time.

Investing implies a preoccupation with capital growth (by buying an asset), while saving implies a concern for accumulating wealth (by lending your money to someone). In the former category, the field is wide open with opportunities, from the stock market to coins and antiques, while the savings field is now enormous, comprising a rapidly growing range of services from banks, building societies, insurance companies, pension funds and so on. Saving implies preserving your capital, while investing implies taking a risk with it to gain an attractive reward.

There are many, many ways of using your money for financial purposes, but the first decision you have to make is whether to put emphasis on capital or on income. If you have a steady job, with a secure future and pension, you may be less concerned to bring in extra income, which can be realised whenever you need it. In this respect, it is important to remember that tying your money up in long-term plans (even including National Savings) or in property or fringe investments can be costly if you want to sell before the end of the allotted investment period or if you have to sell when the market for that particular investment is poor. Indeed, before you buy anything for investment, you should find out exactly how you can sell it again when you want to, and what the financial implications are if you do (like commissions or penalty clauses for early encashment). If, however, you have high income requirements, like a growing family or a large house, you will need to think about obtaining the best deal for a good return, though with less emphasis on capital growth.

The options today are very wide, and in this book we outline all of them. Before you enter any commitment, you should always remember to think through your own financial requirements. Normally, saving money means keeping it readily accessible and this may be attractive to you. But if you invest it, remember also that there is usually a risk-reward connection: the higher the reward, the greater the risk. If you cannot afford to lose the money, do not be tempted to part with it.

## 2  Whose advice should I take?

There are many sources of financial advice, virtually none of them free. Accountancy firms, lawyers, banks, building societies, stockbrokers, antique dealers, insurance brokers – all will offer advice on different aspects of your financial affairs, and some will do it very well. But some will charge directly, others indirectly, and many will be keen to suggest you taking up whatever scheme they are themselves closely involved in. A stockbroker, for example, will often give you good advice as to which shares are good and which to be avoided; but it is a rare one who tells you to forget the stock market and put your money in a bank. This tendency is not to be derided – after all, we are all in business in some form or other – but it is something to be borne in mind when you make decisions about your affairs in the light of what you are being told.

One relatively cheap source of advice is the media – either the financial columns of papers like the *Sunday Telegraph* or *Daily Telegraph*, or the specialist magazines like *Which?* and *Planned Savings*, or radio programmes like the BBC's 'Money Box' – which bring the latest developments in the financial world into perspective. No journalist is infallible (sadly!), and the many columnists in the personal finance field rely heavily on their sources of information. But the quality of assessment and of the writing can be very high, and the independence of papers like the *Telegraph* affords the journalists a unique ability to offer readers a dispassionate and informed guide to available means of savings and investments.

More and more institutions nowadays offer individuals a 'complete' financial planning service, including banks and insurance companies. The barriers between the institutions have been breaking down so fast in recent years that it is difficult to know exactly what is offered by whom, and where the boundaries are. Your local bank manager will buy shares for you, arrange insurance and both lend you money and offer you interest on your own money. But this does not necessarily mean that he is the best person to handle all matters. Banks are very good at many things, like borrowing and lending money and providing a cash transmission service (cheque books and so on), but they are less expert in some other areas, such as, perhaps, trust business.

Lawyers and accountants provide almost the best independent views outside the press, though their opinions are not always expert and they may also have links with particular insurance companies, for example, whereby they receive commission on all policies they arrange. Also, these professionals often charge handsomely for the work that goes with your advice. You may not pay directly for the advice, but you will do so indirectly.

Like so many things in life, personal contact is all important. If you have confidence in your adviser, you will sleep more soundly and probably find the advice is better. There are three lessons:

1. Do not be afraid to shop around. Ask as many people as you want to about the options available to you, and do not worry about asking simple questions. If you have any doubts about your advisers, consult some of the trade associations and institutions listed at the end of the book.

2. Get as much information as you can. By writing, telephoning or visiting, find out all you can about the investment or savings scheme you favour. Read the national press, particularly the *Telegraph* which specialises in this field every day of the week, but concentrates on family and personal finance on Saturdays and Sundays. And write to the press if you have further queries.

3. Remember that whoever's advice you take, the decision is ultimately yours. If things go wrong, you only have yourself to blame – and if they go right, you can take pride in your wisdom.

---

## 3   What are the tax implications of saving and investing?

In every decision to do with your money you need to be aware of your tax position. Changing your finances could severely alter your tax liability, and it is your right to avoid paying tax wherever possible. In the table below we set out the main income tax rates with thresholds, and later on we give details of capital gains, capital transfer and other taxes. We also refer in subsequent sections to the specific tax consequences of certain actions and suggest ways in which tax liabilities can be minimised. Once again, your best bet on the tax front is to take advice from those who know, whether accountants or other professionals.

### Personal tax rates for 1985/6

| Rate (%) | Taxable income (£) |
|---|---|
| 30 | 1 – 16,200 |
| 40 | 16,201 – 19,200 |
| 45 | 19,201 – 24,400 |
| 50 | 24,401 – 32,300 |
| 55 | 32,301 – 40,200 |
| 60 | over 40,200 |

### Do I pay any tax on investment income? 4

As from 1984/85, you will pay no surcharge on investment income. This surcharge, which used to consist of a 15 per cent extra tax on the excess of unearned income over a limit of £7,100 (for 1983/4), was abolished in the March 1984 Budget as part of a wide-ranging reshaping of personal taxation. Investment income will be taxed in the same way as other income, though it may be collected later.

### What is Capital Gains Tax? What are the rates of tax? Would I still pay Capital Gains Tax if my gains are not substantial? 5

Capital Gains Tax (CGT) was first introduced on 1 April 1965. It is completely separate from income tax. Basically, when a 'chargeable person' disposes of a 'chargeable asset' either a 'chargeable gain' or an 'allowable loss' will arise.

If your chargeable gains exceed £5,900 you may be

liable for tax at 30 per cent on the excess (subject to further adjustments explained below). You are a chargeable person if, during the tax year ending 5 April, you dispose of a chargeable asset and are resident in the UK. (If you live outside the UK there are simple rules: you should seek further advice on them.) If you die, all your chargeable assets will be treated as disposed of, but death is not an occasion of charge for CGT purposes. Any form of property in the widest sense, whether situated in the UK or not, can be a chargeable asset. In simple terms, there is a chargeable gain if the proceeds you receive on the disposal of an asset exceed what the asset cost on the date it was acquired: that is, if you buy some shares for £10,000 and sell them for £20,000 there may be a chargeable gain of approximately £10,000. If the proceeds are less than the cost of the asset on acquisition no allowable loss will arise.

There is an annual exemption for capital gains. In 1985/6, if your aggregate chargeable gains do not exceed £5,900 you do not pay any CGT.

In addition, there is an adjustment for inflation to the value of each asset you sell. The Retail Price Index is used as the measure of inflation in this case, and this "indexation" allowance applies from the moment the asset was acquired or March 1982 – whichever is later.

In the 1985 Budget, the Chancellor also allowed the indexation provision to apply to losses as well as gains.

## 6 Are any assets exempt from Capital Gains Tax?

Gains arising on the disposal of certain assets, listed below, are exempt; by the same token any loss arising on their disposal is not allowable for these purposes.

**Chattels:** These are assets which are touchable ('tangible') and moveable. They are exempt if the disposal is for £3,000 or less. (A special computation is necessary if the sum exceeds £3,000.) This does not apply to currency (but see under **Foreign currency** below). There are also special rules dealing with 'sets' of chattels.

**Motor cars:** These are not chargeable assets unless they are of a type not commonly used as a private vehicle and unsuitable to be so used.

**National Savings Certificates, Premium Bonds, etc:** These and other government securities which are not transferable are exempt whenever they are acquired or disposed of.

**Government securities ('Gilt-edged'):** These are exempt if held for more than 12 months.

**Betting and other winnings:** Winnings from betting are not chargeable gains. Premium Bond winnings, etc., are also exempt.

**Foreign currency:** This is exempt when disposed of providing it was acquired only for personal and family expenditure.

**Medals and decorations:** These are exempt unless acquired by purchase.

**Compensation for damages:** This is exempt if received for personal or professional wrong or injury; if the damages, etc., relate to an asset, payment will constitute a disposal.

**Life assurance policies and deferred annuities:** These are exempt when they are disposed of or realised by the original policy-holder but *not* when they are disposed of or realised by another person who may have acquired them by subsequent purchase.

**Your home:** Generally speaking if your home is your only or main residence throughout your period of ownership there will be no charge to CGT when you sell the property. This exemption extends to the building and in most cases up to one acre of land.

---

**7 What is Capital Transfer Tax? What are the rates of tax? When am I liable to pay it?**

Capital Transfer Tax (CTT) was introduced in 1974 to replace estate duty, which only taxed assets passing on death and certain lifetime gifts. CTT is charged on the value transferred by a chargeable transfer, whether it is made during a lifetime or on death. A transfer of value is, broadly, anything which results in a reduction to the person making the transfer. The value transferred is the resulting fall in value in the estate of the person making the transfer. A chargeable transfer is any transfer of value made by an individual after 26 March 1974. For CTT purposes, 'estate' means the aggregate of all the property to which you are beneficially entitled.

Unlike CGT, for the purposes of CTT, death is an occasion of charge. There are two separate scales for the rates of tax, one for transfers made during your lifetime and the other for all your property which is transferred on the event of your death. There is an added sting in the tail, since any transfers you make in the three years prior to your death are charged at the 'death' rates, which are considerably higher than the 'lifetime' rates – though credit is given for tax already paid. Remember that this is a cumulative tax and that your transfers are therefore added to each other, year by year.

This may seem a rather black picture, but perhaps the situation is not as bad as it first seems. You do not start paying CTT until your chargeable transfers have totalled £67,000, this being in addition to the annual and other exemptions covered below. For the purposes of CTT, husband and wife are treated separately so you will each have a total of £67,000 chargeable transfers before you pay this tax.

Furthermore, for transfers made on or after March 1981, the cumulative principle applies only to transfers made in the ten years before the transfer in question in determining the amount of tax to be paid on that occasion. This has the effect of reinstating the £67,000 non-chargeable band every ten years.

## CTT rates

| Band of chargeable value £'000 | | Rate on death per cent | Lifetime rate per cent |
|---|---|---|---|
| Over | Not over | | |
| 0 – | 67 | Nil | Nil |
| 67 – | 89 | 30 | 15 |
| 89 – | 122 | 35 | 17½ |
| 122 – | 155 | 40 | 20 |
| 155 – | 194 | 45 | 22½ |
| 194 – | 243 | 50 | 25 |
| 243 – | 299 | 55 | 27½ |
| 299 | | 60 | 30 |

For these tax questions, we are grateful to the authors of the Sunday Telegraph book *101 Ways of Saving Tax*, which is a comprehensive guide to every aspect of taxation.

# II
# Saving your money

**8    Should I put my money in the bank?**

Nowadays, most of us have bank accounts, and if not a
bank account, then a building society account. Between them, the banks and the building societies hold
the vast majority of savings in the UK.

The basic principle of a bank is that it will make a
profit for itself by borrowing money from one person
and lending it to another. The major clearing banks
have developed into vast organisations with many
thousands of branches, each offering a wide range of
services. But their bread and butter is the taking of
deposits, whether from the individual or from large
corporations, and the lending of that money to someone else *at a profit*. For the individual the advantage of
having a bank account is that he or she will be able to
use the wide range of bank services on offer (and particularly the transmission of money by using cheque
books and credit cards). There are two major types of
accounts offered by the clearing banks. The first is the
current account, which pays no interest, but which
allows the individual to write cheques against his balance. The second is the seven-day deposit account
which pays an interest rate broadly in line with market
rates, but for which the individual has to give seven
days' notice of withdrawal.

There are other options open to you, particularly
among the more enterprising building societies, but

everybody who wants to have an intelligent arrangement of his or her financial affairs should have a bank account. The payment of salary cheques by monthly direct credit is one obvious advantage of having a current account. But whether it is worth putting a substantial portion of your money into the seven-day deposit account depends very much on how competitive the banks interest rate is. It goes without saying that, even though the banks have started to penalise customers with less than a minimum of £100 or £500 in their current account, it is not a good idea to hold any significant sum in a current account, because it pays no interest. Individuals should be prepared to move their money between accounts, to get the best rate possible.

Of course, you have to bear in mind your relationship with your bank manager in case you want to borrow money or use other bank services at some time. In this case you may decide to have available both a clearing bank current account and a seven-day deposit account, even though you may have other savings options. Generally speaking, the rates banks pay on seven-day deposit money are competitive with other options. Interest is paid gross i.e. without deduction of tax.

Apart from the simple current and deposit accounts, all the clearing banks have a wide range of savings schemes offering different benefits. It is impossible to list here all the schemes offered by the clearing banks let alone those of the trustee savings banks, the merchant banks and other banking insitutions. But the clearers all provide the options of saving money for longer periods, thus earning higher interest rates, and of saving in regular instalments. The clearing banks are highly competitive with each other, but tend to offer the same range of services. You have to decide in what form you want to save your money, and whether or not to choose some of the more complicated schemes.

**9    How safe is the money I leave in the bank?**

Nothing in life is absolutely certain, but investing
money in a major clearing bank must be as safe a risk as
anything could be. Since 1979 the Bank of England has
supervised the British banking system, under the
Banking Act. This divides institutions into two
categories – recognised banks and licensed deposit tak-
ers. To get on to either list various criteria have to be
met, and above all the Bank of England has to be
satisfied that the institution is sound. It goes without
saying that the clearing banks are very much at the top
of the top category.

In addition, the Banking Act introduced a deposit
protection scheme which effectively protects 75 per
cent of the first £10,000 of any bank deposit. The
scheme is financed by contribution (0.01 per cent of the
sterling deposit base) from each banking institution on
the list. It is hoped that this will be enough to deal with
any crisis that the authorities can foresee.

**10    Should I stick only to the clearing banks?**

The clearing banks are the largest banking institutions
and they comprise Barclays, Lloyds, National Westminster, Midland and Williams and Glyn's in England
and Wales, and Clydesdale Bank, Royal Bank of Scotland and Bank of Scotland in Scotland. As explained
above, the clearing bank has many advantages over the
non-clearing bank in the range of services offered but
there are several other kinds of banking institution
(other than building societies which are dealt with
below) which can offer the saver some interesting
options.

**1 Trustee Savings Banks** The TSBs started many
years ago as a collection of regional savings banks which

were originally restricted only to simple investment schemes for the small saver. But in recent years they have been changing their constitutions with a view to becoming a public limited company soon. The sixteen regional TSBs make up the fifth largest of the high street banks with customer deposits of more than £6 billion and over 1,600 branches. In fact, in terms of sheer numbers of accounts, with more than 13 million active accounts on their books the TSBs form the leading personal banking group in the UK. The TSBs offer a wide range of services including cheques, savings, investment and other deposit accounts, and special high-interest schemes for longer-term savers. There are plans under way for six-day banking and out-of-hours cash service. For straightforward deposits and cheque book business the TSBs offer just as good a savings opportunity as the leading clearing banks. Like the clearers, they pay no interest on current accounts, and pay similar rates on deposit accounts. Indeed, because they have traditionally been concerned with small savings accounts they are particularly suitable for this kind of service. They now offer the TSB trust card to members of the VISA system. You will perhaps not get the variety of service that is available to the large clearers, particularly on commercial business, but in interest rates and services offered to the small saver the TSBs are very competitive.

2 **The merchant banks** Many of the merchant banks, which developed this century as institutions specialising in servicing the needs of companies, now have a range of facilities for the individual. If you are worth several hundred thousand pounds, or a million or more, you will find these merchant banks will be the perfect source of advice and investment opportunities of all kinds, as they have some well-qualified staff with a deep knowledge of financial markets. If, though, you have less spare cash than that, you will normally find

that they will not go out of their way to encourage you to become a client. However, in the last couple of years some, such as Schroders and Robert Fleming, have introduced special schemes to attract the small saver, including interest-bearing current accounts. Others, such as Hill Samuel, have regional offices in several cities, in which individual accounts are encouraged as much as corporate accounts. One disadvantage is that, though some of these banks supply cheque books, these may not be recognised by shops and traders. An advantage is that, in some cases, the interest rates they offer may be higher.

**3 Foreign banks** In the last few years the number of foreign banks in Britain has doubled to well over 350. Although most of them are here for currency business, many also compete with British banks for Sterling business. Not all are looking for individual customers, but many of them are, such as the large American banks like Chase Manhattan, Citibank, Bank of America, and so on. Broadly speaking, the interest rates and the benefits of having an account with these banks will be similar to those offered by the British banks. Many have their own individual schemes and some may not be interested in you unless you can make a substantial deposit with them. But with some of their services, like mortgages, they can occasionally be more imaginative than the British banks and will often be more aggresive about marketing their facilities. These foreign banks are almost all based in London, though some have branches in regional cities.

**4 The Co-op Bank** This bank has grown out of the co-operative movement in this country, which has its roots in trade unionism and the Labour Party, although the links are now not as strong as they were. The Co-op Bank offers a wide range of personal banking services, though without the large bank network of the clearing banks. Nevertheless, it does offer a useful alternative.

**5 The Girobank** This is a banking service operated throughout the Post Office and its 21,000 branches. It also offers the saver some simple savings schemes, at competitive interest rates, though it does not naturally have the same breadth of operations as the large banks.

## What are the advantages of building societies? 11

At present there are around 11,250 branches of banks in England and Wales, with a further 1,500 in Scotland. The 'Big Four' London clearing banks alone hold just over £60 billion of Sterling deposits including some £21 billion of current account money. By contrast, the Building Societies Association (BSA) with 172 members and 6,500 branches throughout the country has a total of some £70 billion of customer deposits. The object of building societies is to provide finance for home ownership, and with this in mind the Government has maintained a system of tax relief available for the societies in the services they offer. Building societies are not run like banks – they are non profit-making bodies, effectively owned by their investors who can vote at annual meetings on whatever matters of society are put before them. They are specifically prohibited from making loans which are not connected with house finance. The money for this vast amount of mortgage lending comes from savers' deposits with the societies which are normally in the form of share accounts, i.e. money can be withdrawn at short notice like a current account in the bank. But, unlike current accounts, share accounts pay interest with tax already deducted. This makes them very competitive with bank deposit rates, and explains why in the last ten years there has been such a strong growth in societies' deposits.

In addition to the share account, most societies offer a fixed term account for higher interest rates, also with tax deducted. In recent years, the societies have become much more aggressive in marketing their services and broadening the range of facilities they offer. Several have cash dispensers, some have linked up with banks to provide cheque books or credit cards, and some offer insurance related schemes. A recent report by a group of societies in the BSA proposed that they should be allowed to act as estate agents, acquire an interest in a bank or insurance company, make personal loans, carry out surveys of land for development, operate in EEC countries and offer index-linked mortgages. These radical proposals will take some years to bear fruit but they illustrate how barriers are breaking down in the high street.

One advantage that the building societies have over the banks is opening hours. Most societies are open from 9 to 5 on weekdays and at least part of the day on Saturday (by contrast, the banks close business at 3 or 3.30 p.m. and only some of them open on Saturdays). Because the societies are concerned primarily with the small saver, they are limited to £30,000 maximum for individual savings deposited. A saver is well advised to have an account at a building society in addition to a bank account, to be able to take advantage of any new schemes either may introduce.

## 12  Is it worth taking out other regular savings schemes?

Apart from investing particular sums of money in one or more of the savings schemes which are available to the public, you would be well advised to consider one of the long-term savings schemes on offer. These provide opportunities to put away money on a regular basis without reducing too greatly your regular income. And in some cases the Government offers tax advantages for the saver. Wage earners contribute to government welfare schemes through the regular contributions they make to the National Insurance Scheme. Benefits they receive from the State include pensions, free medical care on the National Health Service and unemployment benefit if they are out of work. But many individuals find it useful to supplement their pension for example, by contributing to a company scheme (over which normally they have little control) or a self-employed pension scheme. You would be well advised to consider this.

## Should I change my pension arrangements? What if I am self-employed? 13

An individual's pension is often his or her only asset although he or she may spend little time increasing it. But there are pitfalls to watch out for. Britain's pension fund industry is now worth a massive £80 billion and has grown swiftly. The principal anomaly in the pensions field is the inequitable treatment meted out by funds to 'early leavers', i.e. those who move jobs or are made redundant and leave much of their unclaimed benefits in the fund from which they are departing. One way out of the early leavers' dilemma has come from a number of insurance companies, who offer independent pension plans or 'buy-out' bonds under which a lump sum is transferred out of the pension fund into the company, and invested to produce either a pension or another lump sum on retirement. Insurance companies offering this include Crown Life, Equitable Life, and London and Manchester Assurance. Although guarantees are less than those under the deferred pension (which is related to the contributions he made before leaving the firm), the scope for growth of the investments may more than make up the difference.

For the self-employed things are very different. To get more than your basic state pension (£52.55 for a married couple at the time of writing) self-employed people need to make their own arrangements and seek advice from professional advisers (such as Towry Law and Noble Lowndes). The advantages for self-employed people making extra pension provision are far-reaching. Tax relief on contributions is given at the top rate of income tax paid, while investment in tax-free pension funds ensures a much greater potential growth than taxed investment. At retirement a tax-free lump sum is available and the pension is taxed as earned rather than unearned income.

There are two main types of pension plan for the self-employed: with profits and unit-linked. Most popular are the with-profits contracts which provide guaranteed minimum benefits together with annual bonuses which will vary according to the profits from investment. Unit-linked plans can be more risky because their value fluctuates with the stock markets, but they do offer the potential for higher gains. The best approach is to spread contributions between both types of policy. Choosing the right insurance company is the hardest part of the exercise and it can make a considerable difference to the results. A survey by the specialist *Planned Savings* magazine showed that the worst performing company paid around half as much pension as the best, from an equal start. A 65-year-old man retiring in 1982 who took out a with-profits pension policy in 1972 saving £500 a year would have got a pension of £1,724 per annum from the top-performing Equitable Life, but only £912 per annum from Gresham Life. Past performance is a good guide to the better companies, and some of the best-known City names recur year by year in the lists of top companies and fund managers. In the with-profits fields, Equitable Life, Prudential, Norwich Union and Scottish

Widows are prominent; while the newer unit-linked schemes are offered by M & G, Hambro Life, Vanbrugh and others. A registered insurance broker will advise you on the best choice.

## Should I take out an annuity? 14

An annuity is essentially a scheme whereby an individual receives annual payments after retirement age having invested a capital sum at some time before retirement. The 'purchased life' annuities operate so that where an individual invests some of his capital in an annuity, he receives the payments at a later date and part of the payment is treated as the return of his capital and so is not taxed. The remainder is taxed as unearned income. The split between capital and income will depend on the individual's age at the date of purchasing the annuity. It is also possible for an individual over 65 to borrow on the security of his house, and providing at least 90 per cent of the loan is used to buy an annuity for himself (or jointly with his wife) he can obtain some tax relief on the interest paid. Details of such annuity schemes can be obtained from the major life assurance companies or investment advisers. They are worth considering for anyone concerned about retirement, though they need to be looked at in conjunction with other pension arrangements.

## Should I take out a life assurance policy? 15

As from March 1984, new-life assurance policies are not eligible for tax relief on the premiums paid. Previously all premiums payable were eligible for 15 per cent tax relief, and the Chancellor has stipulated that all existing policies will continue to be eligible for such relief. The change only affects those policies taken out after March 13, 1984.

However, it still may be worthwhile taking out a life assurance policy for the obvious advantages of providing cover against death, particularly for those with families, and offering a useful means of long-term savings. All the major insurance companies, including the Prudential, General Accident, Hambro Life and so on, offer life policies. It is better to stick to these larger groups rather than the smaller less well-known firms.

# III
# NATIONAL SAVINGS

## What forms of National Savings are there? 16

The Government offers the public many forms of savings and investments – through the National Savings movement and through the financial markets. For example, government bonds and treasury bills can be bought in the city through stockbrokers and money market operators respectively. These are described in more detail in Chapter IV. The range of savings offered by the Government is wide, since in the last few years it has decided to finance a larger share of its borrowing needs through National Savings rather than mainly through the sale of government bonds to the markets. All the options available at the time of writing are described here. Further details are obtainable from most post offices, the Bonds and Stocks Office or the National Savings Department Head Office.

## How can I open an account with the National Savings Bank? 17

There are two principal accounts: an ordinary account and an investment account. An *ordinary account* offers interest (at the time of writing) of 6 per cent on a balance above £5,000 and 3 per cent below, with the first £70 per annum of interest paid tax-free. Husbands and wives are each entitled to this £70 tax-free interest. Interest is earned on each pound held on deposit for complete calendar months. Money does not earn interest in the month of deposit or in the month in which it is withdrawn. You can open an ordinary account with £1, and the upper limit is normally £10,000. You may withdraw up to £100 on demand at any Savings Bank Post Office during normal shopping hours, including Saturday mornings. Regular customers can exceed the withdrawal limits at a named post office. You can withdraw £250 cash at this chosen post office but to qualify for this you must have used an ordinary account at this post office for at least six months. There are facilities for standing orders and payment of bills up to £250.

The *investment account* offers (at the time of writing) 12¼ per cent calculated on the same basis as the ordinary account. The interest rate varies according to general conditions in the financial markets, and the latest rate can be discovered by telephoning the 24-hour answering service:

*South*: London (01-603 8646/8672)
*North*: Lytham St Annes (0253 723714)
*Scotland*: Glasgow (041-632 2766)

The upper limit on investment accounts is £200,000 with a £1 minimum. The interest is automatically credited to accounts on December 31st each year and is paid gross (i.e. without tax deducted at source).

To open either kind of account, you simply need to fill out a straightforward application form at a post office. Accounts can be opened for young children (although withdrawals are not normally allowed before the child is 7), by two or more people jointly, and for other parties in trust.

In many ways these accounts are similar to those available from the major high street banks; the disadvantage is that there is no cheque book, although the advantage is that the accounts are available throughout 20,000 post offices with longer opening hours than the banks.

### What are the advantages of National Savings Income Bonds? 18

Income bonds can be purchased by individuals or their children, by friendly or provident societies, by clubs and funds, by charities, by registered companies and by trustees. They offer monthly income payments at a competitive interest rate (currently 11 per cent) and access to capital at any time on three- or six-months notice. Your first investment must be at least £2,000. Larger purchases and additions to existing holdings are in multiples of £1,000. The maximum holding is £200,000. Interest which is paid in full without deductions of tax, is calculated on a day-to-day basis from the date your payment is received at the Bonds and Stocks Office. The bonds may be held for a usual guarantee period of ten years from the first interest date after purchase. To buy bonds, ask for the combined application form and prospectus at the post office.

### Should I buy ordinary National Savings Certificates? 19

National Savings Certificates offer tax-free capital gains over a short-term period, which is normally five years. Issues of certificates are normally held open for a limited period of several months, before being closed when a new issue which takes account of changes in interest rates is introduced. For example, the 30th issue of certificates, which was on offer in the summer of 1983, offered a return equivalent to a compound annual interest rate of 8.85 per cent over the full five years. A £100 purchase after five years would increase to £152.84.

An individual may hold up to £5,000 of the 30th issue, in addition to all other holdings of National Savings Certificates. (This maximum amount varies with each issue.) The certificates can be bought in denominations of one, two, four, ten, twenty, forty and eighty units of £25 each. You can cash in your certificates at any time but the repayment value increases only at the end of each year, and the longer you hold them the more the value increases. Any saver or investor would be well advised to put some money into this simple tax-free form of investment.

## 20 Are index-linked National Savings Certificates a good idea?

Recently the Government has made available to everybody index-linked National Savings Certificates which are designed to protect lump-sum savings from the effects of inflation and anybody of any age can now buy up to £10,000-worth. These certificates are proofed against inflation; once you have held them for a full year their cash value will then rise along with inflation over the past twelve months, and their value from month to month will depend on the monthly changes in prices as measured by the Retail Prices Index. Repayments of these certificates are free of all income tax and CGT.

Someone who bought in or after November 1982 and before October 1983 would be credited with a supplement of 0.2 per cent of the purchase price for each calendar month up to the end of October 1983. This supplement was then index-linked and will be paid when the certificates are cashed, provided they have been held at least for a year. After five years the repayment value will increase by a bonus of 4 per cent of the purchase price, which is in addition to the index-linked increase and the supplement. Obviously, if the rate of inflation falls, these certificates become less attractive compared with other savings opportunities, but it is certainly worth a saver with funds to spare putting at least some of his or her money in this inflation-proofed form. After all, no one knows what will happen to inflation in the years to come.

---

### Is it worth trying to win money on Premium Bonds? 21

Every month the National Savings computer, known as ERNIE, chooses a large number of prizes from the millions of individual bonds that are registered in the computer's memory. The top monthly payment is £250,000 and there are weekly jackpot prizes of £100,000, £50,000 and £25,000. There are also five prizes of £10,000 every month, fifty prizes of £5,000, 250 prizes of £1,000, 750 prizes of £500, 250,000 prizes of £100 and 75,000 prizes of £50. Premium Bonds can be bought at post offices and banks in multiples of £5, which give you five separate chances of a prize in every draw up to £10,000 maximum. Anyone over 16 can buy the bonds, and under-16s can have bonds bought for them by parents, guardians or grandparents. When you win a prize the Bonds and Stocks Office will write to you with the good news at the last address you gave them, and most daily newspapers publish the numbers of the high-value winning bonds. All prizes are tax-free. The money you invest in Premium Bonds pays no interest but you can get your money back at any time by filling out a withdrawal form at any post office.

---

### Should I take advantage of index-linked Save As You Earn? 22

SAYE is a National Savings scheme designed to protect the purchasing power of regular monthly savings. You agree to make sixty regular monthly contributions over five years and each contribution will be adjusted in line with whatever change in prices had occured between the making of the contribution and the completion of the agreement. Anyone over 16 can use SAYE and you do not have to be a wage earner. The amount of monthly contributions can be anything from £4 to £50, but must remain the same throughout the five years of the contract. There was a 0.2 per cent supplement for new contracts up to November 1983. Like other index-linked opportunities this means of savings becomes attractive when inflation is on the increase and every saver would do well to have a little money tied up in SAYE.

---

**23 Is it worth buying government stock through the National Savings scheme register?**

The quickest way to buy and sell government bonds, otherwise known as 'gilt-edged' stock, is through a stockbroker, who will act for you in the stock market. Alternatively, you could buy gilt-edged stock through a bank or other similar agent, but this will involve paying a commission, even though quite a small one (see Question 28). There are commission charges on buying government bonds through the National Savings scheme register, but they tend to be smaller than those charged by stockbrokers. The charges are £1 for sums up to £250, and a further 50p for every additional £125. On sales, the charge is 10p for every £10 up to £100, £1 for anything between £100 and £250, and an additional 50p for every extra £125. The general rule is that gilts may be held by anyone and are subject to no CGT if they are held for more than twelve months. Dividend payments are normally made every six months and are paid without deduction of tax. If you wish to buy gilts by this method, fill in the investment application form GS1(G) (available from post offices) for each stock you wish to buy, and send it in the green envelope G53M to the Bonds and Stocks Office, Blackpool, Lancashire, with a cheque made out to the Director of Savings.

Note that gilts purchased through a broker or bank cannot be sold through the National Savings Scheme register. This method of buying gilts may be useful if you have no connections with a stockbroker or bank and are not worried about buying at the best possible price. One disadvantage is that buying and selling orders can take a few days to complete because of postage delays and you cannot be sure of the exact price you will pay. But you may pay less commission.

# IV
# Stocks and shares

## 24  What are the best ways of investing in stocks and shares?

For those who do not want to simply put their money in
the bank or take advantage of the many savings
schemes, investing in stocks and shares provides an
opportunity either for long-term capital growth or for
short-term gains, with the attendant possibility of loss
as well as profit. Essentially, buying shares means buying a 'security' in a company, or a share in the equity,
which is not redeemable or repayable in any form, but
may carry a dividend each year depending on the company's performance. The idea is that a well-managed
company will continue to increase its profits each year
and that it will therefore be able to increase the
dividend and, along with that, the value of its shares.

By and large a company which sets up in business
will raise a certain amount of money by issuing shares
and a larger amount by other means, including borrowing from the bank or in the form of a fixed-interest debt
of a fixed maturity (i.e. a debt which will have to be
repaid within a certain time, such as five or fifteen
years). Because shares have no ultimate value, they can
increase to astronomical levels if a company is doing
well. They can also lose all their value if it falls on hard
times. Fixed-interest debt (such as bonds carrying an
interest payment of, say, 10 per cent a year) is repayable
at a known time and thus its value can be more easily
defined. The government bond market, for example,

contains a vast amount of fixed interest bonds which have been issued by the government, and their value can be more or less fixed within certain boundaries because the money will ultimately be repaid at face value.

Larger companies have shares which are 'quoted' on the stock market, i.e. they are bought and sold every day in the market place and they are held by a wide range of investors. By far the best way of buying shares is through the stock market, through a stockbroking firm which will charge a commission every time you buy and sell. There are other ways of investing in companies, such as buying shares in private companies, but you can normally only do this through personal contact, and there is no guarantee that you will be able to sell the shares when you want to.

Stock Exchange companies are subject to rules and regulations laid down by the Exchange itself, thus they should be safer than non-quoted companies. But when the climate is gloomy for the market as a whole, or when particular troubles strike a company, the shares can fall sharply. For leading shares, such as ICI, British Petroleum, Glaxo and so on, investment can be a good long-term proposition – as government bonds can be also. Fortunes can be made and lost on the smaller shares. Investors can make good money on the stock market, but they should be aware of the risks. If you want to invest directly in the stock market and have not done so before, contact either a stockbroker (of which there are many listed at the end of this book) or a bank which can place the order for you. If you have any other general queries, contact the Stock Exchange direct.

Another way of investing in the stock market is through unit trusts or investment trusts, and we examine these methods in some detail later on. Unit trusts in particular offer the chance of spreading your risk (while limiting your possible gains or losses) and giving the key decisions to someone else, the manager of the individual trust. To find out which are the best trusts, read the *Daily Telegraph* (especially on Saturday) and the *Sunday Telegraph*, which are acknowledged as leaders among the national press covering this field.

## 25   How does the Stock Exchange work?

According to the Exchange's own history, the market evolved in London during the seventeenth century from informal gatherings of stock and share dealers in the coffee houses around the Royal Exchange. In the nineteenth century other stock exchanges opened up outside London, and in 1965 these, together with London, formed a Federation of Stock Exchanges in Great Britain and Ireland. In 1973 they joined together to form the Stock Exchange. Today it is made up of some 4,200 individual members, each of whom must be 21 or over and must have at least three years' experience with a member firm. There are 252 member firms, of whom 17 are jobbers (firms that make markets in shares, buying and selling on their own account) and the rest are brokers (who buy and sell on behalf of clients such as the largest investment institutions and private individuals, but do not deal on their own account). Roughly 7,400 securities are officially listed on the Stock Exchange, 2,025 of which represent the equity capital of British companies, many of quite modest size. The rest are a large mixture of overseas securities, bonds and government and other public sector stocks. There are probably some two million individuals in Britain who own shares, with direct private clients accounting for roughly 35 per cent by value of all deals or bargains made on the Stock Exchange in equities. About 10 per cent of bargains are for clients of the main clearing banks, who receive a share of the broker's commission for their services.

The way the market works is that brokers carry out the buying and selling of orders on behalf of their clients by going onto the floor of the Exchange in London's Throgmorton Street, and finding the best price from the jobbers who are dealing in that particular share. Prices can move quickly according to economic or political developments, or announcements concerning the share in question. Investors are well advised to keep an eye on their share prices by reading the financial press. Some speculative shares, like Poseidon over a decade ago (which moved from several pence to £120 before falling back again), and, in 1982/83, Polly Peck and London and Liverpool Trust (which both soared before tumbling), can make money for the quick-footed. By all means have a go at these if you can afford it, but do not be too greedy. Remember those market maxims: 'It is never wrong to take a profit' and 'Always leave a little profit for the next man'.

---

**What procedures are involved?** 26

The market operates on a system of fortnightly accounts (or ten working days). On the day that he deals for you, the broker will send you a contract note, which sets out the details of the transaction – the full title of the security involved, the amount bought and the price. The number of shares multiplied by the price gives the consideration on which broker's commission and transfer stamp duty (if applicable; see Question 28) are based. Until the share certificate is sent to you, which may take some six or eight weeks from the day of dealing, the contract note is evidence of ownership. Your contract note also includes the date by which you are due to pay your broker. In the case of government stock, it is usually the day after dealing. For company securities, it will normally be two or three weeks later. For overseas stock a variety of different times apply, but the appropriate date will always be shown on the contract note.

Much of the paper work is speeded up by the Stock Exchange's computer system, known as TALISMAN, which keeps track of shares passing through the settlement process. If the company in question has announced a dividend to which you are entitled, but it has, because of the delay in arranging registration, gone to the previous owner of the shares, your broker will claim it on your behalf. To avoid the need for this as far as possible, the Stock Exchange marks shares 'ex-dividend' some weeks before payment is due.

The procedure for selling is much the same as that for buying. Again, your broker will send you a contract note, but he will also enclose a transfer form for you to sign. This, together with your share certificate, must be returned to him in time for the settlement day shown on the contract note.

---

## 27 What protection does an investor have against his or her broker running into trouble?

To protect investors, the Stock Exchange has set up a compensation fund to recompense clients who lose money on stock as a result of their broker defaulting. Payments from this fund are entirely a decision of the Stock Exchange Council, and, while it is rare for a claim to be refused, compensation is not automatic. The Council does not replace securities which have been misappropriated, as compensation is always given in money form. Normally this represents the market value of the securities at the time of the default. Full details of this fund are obtainable from the Stock Exchange.

## What are the costs of dealing? 28

The system of 'fixed' commissions is due to be phased
out by 1986 under a recent agreement between the
Government and the Stock Exchange. Commission
charges on dealings in shares are listed below, but are
likely to be adjusted in 1985. From April 1984 commissions on dealings in Gilts are as follows:

### Stockbrokers' commission charges
*Gilts*
i.   Securities having no final redemption date
     within ten years:
     0.8%    on the first £2,500 consideration
     0.25%   on the next £15,500
     0.125%  on the next £232,000
     0.1%    on the next £750,000
     0.09%   on the next £3,000,000
     0.04%   on the next £6,000,000
     0.2%    on the excess
ii.  Securities having ten years or less
     to final redemption:
     0.8%      on the first £2,500
     0.12%     on the next £15,500
     0.0625%   on the next £232,000
     0.05%     on the next £750,000
     0.02%     on the next £6,000,000
     0.01%     on the excess
iii. Securities having five years or less to
     final redemption and not in default:
     At discretion

*Shares*
     1.65%    on the first £7,000
     0.55%    on the next £8,000
     0.5%     on the next £115,000

0.4%    on the next £170,000
0.3%    on the next £600,000
0.2%    on the next £1,100,000
0.125% on the excess

In addition transactions in securities are normally subject to government stamp duty of 1 per cent paid by the purchaser. This stamp duty is payable on all equities, and on stocks with an equity element, but it is *not* payable on government stocks or corporate bonds.

## 29   Is it worth dealing within the account?

If you both buy and sell an equity during the fortnightly accounting period, then you will not have to pay stamp duty. The duty will be charged on your first contract note but will be deducted on your second. Also, you will normally only pay one commission charge to your broker instead of two. These concessions are possible because the stock in question has not officially been transferred to you. You can use this facility to deal in shares without actually paying for them, but it goes without saying that there can be substantial risks involved in this.

## 30   What is the traded option market? Is it worth investing in it?

One way of investing in the stock market is through traded options. These give the investor the possibility of a much greater gain when a share price moves, but also of losing all his money quite easily. The idea of the option is to give the investor the right to buy or sell a certain amount of a particular share at an agreed price and within a stated period. If the option-holder does not exercise his rights during the period of the option – because he decides it would not be in his interest to do so – then the option ceases to exist. On the Stock Exchange 'call options' give the holder the right to purchase shares in the underlying securities at an agreed price, known as the 'exercise price'. 'Put' options carry the right to sell shares. Each traded option contract normally represents an option of 1,000 shares of the underlying security. These contracts can then be bought and sold in the market independent of what is happening to the underlying share. For example, if an investor purchases an International Manufacturing July 300 contract at a price of 14p, this would give him the right to buy 1,000 shares in this company at 300p each at any time until the expiry date in July. Let us assume that the shares currently stand in the market at 290p. At some stage they rise to 319p – the options might then well move from the original 14p to 28p. In this way a 10 per cent rise in the share price can be equivalent to a 100 per cent rise in the option price. Of course, if the price of the share falls and stays well below 300p the option may become worthless.

People who sell options initially are known as 'option writers' and are entitled to receive the premium paid by the buyer on the first day of business. They commit themselves to delivering shares in the underlying security at the exercise price at the specified future date. The economics of writing an option are simple – the investor deposits share certificates with his broker to cover the number of shares represented by the contracts before or at the same time as he instructs him to write the options on his behalf. As an alternative to depositing share certificates, there are certain types of collateral which may be put up, such as gilt edged stock or cash. Profits arise from dealing in traded options are subject to CGT.

**Commissions on London traded options (£ sterling)**
£1.50 per option contract plus *ad valorem* commission of:

    2.5% on the first £5,000 option money
    1.5% on the next £5,000 option money
    1.0% on the excess

The minimum commission to be charged on business in London traded options in Sterling is:

    (a) in transactions of £20 or less option money: at discretion.

    (b) on transactions of more than £20 option money: £10 overall with a minimum of £5 *ad valorem* commission or at the scale laid down, whichever is the greater.

---

### 31   What is the Unlisted Securities Market? Does it offer the chance to make money?

In 1980, the Stock Exchange recognised the need for the addition of a junior section to the market; which would allow small companies to raise finance by issuing shares without going through the more stringent requirements that are involved in a full listing. The result is that companies which are traded on the USM are mostly smaller, younger and with less shares on the market than fully-listed stocks. They are therefore more speculative. Commissions on USM dealings are the same as other Stock Exchange share deals, and the procedures are the same.

There are over 250 companies traded on the USM, compared with 23 in 1980. Because the risks are generally greater on the USM, the shares stand at a higher rating (measured by the ratio of share price to the company's profits) than non-USM companies and can move sharply up. In the first half of 1983 a lot of money was made by investors on the USM as a result of these factors. There may well be more such opportunities ahead, but investors should be aware that the same factors which can exaggerate a price rise on the USM may later lead to a sharper fall than normal.

---

### Can I deal in stocks and shares outside the Stock Exchange? 32

There are a few firms, mainly in the City of London, who deal in stocks and shares on an 'over-the-counter' (OTC) basis, i.e. they sell them to individuals and institutions much like consumer goods are sold across shop counters. But these are shares which, though technically issued by public companies, are for most purposes private, and thus are normally controlled by families or individuals. And of course they are not traded on the official stock market.

The oldest OTC market is that run by Granville and Co., which is both a licensed dealer in securities and a licensed deposit-taker. Its market works on the principle of matching buyers and sellers, and it does not itself take a position. Another leading market-maker in OTC stocks is Harvard Securities, which takes the opposite approach and runs its own books in stocks, which, it argues, makes for an easier marketplace. Any licensed dealer in securities (licensed by the Department of Trade) can sell stocks to the public. If you wish to buy stocks on this market, be sure you find out in some detail about the company whose shares you buy. One advantage of investing in a *new* issue of shares on the OTC markets is that the money you put in may qualify for tax relief under the Business Expansion Scheme. This does not apply to stock exchange issues, even on the USM.

## 33   Should I buy unit trusts?

One easy and very popular way for the small investor to put money into the stock market is by buying unit trusts. These provide a means of investing in shares without buying the shares themselves. They are particularly suitable for people who have neither the time nor the money, nor perhaps the expertise, to undertake direct investment in equities successfully. On another level, they also provide a route into specialist and overseas markets.

The concept on which unit trusts are based is extremely simple. Large numbers of investors pool their money in order to obtain a spread of stock market investments. The trust is divided into equal portions called units. The price of the units is calculated usually every day by the managers, rather than being determined by supply and demand in the market. Two prices are quoted for unit trusts – the high (offer) price being the price the investor pays to buy units, and the low (bid) price being the one he will reserve for units to sell back to the managers. Unit trust managers are the only ones who are allowed to make a market in unit trust units. They must be prepared to buy units from the public and sell to them at any time. The price of units is governed by the underlying securities of a fund. The price therefore fluctuates with movements of the market in which a fund is invested. The value of an investor holding in a unit trust can therefore go down as well as up.

**Initial and annual charges** The unit trust charging system consists of an initial charge and an annual management charge. The initial charge is included in the price at which managers will sell units to the public, and the annual charge is normally taken out of the income of the trust fund. The charge is subject to VAT at 15 per cent but the initial charge is not. There is no

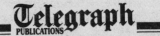

upper limit on the charges that unit trust managers can levy on the unit holders, except that laid down in the trust deed. Although there is no agreed policy, the charges which have emerged since controls were removed as being generally acceptable are a 5 per cent initial charge and a corresponding annual charge of $\frac{1}{4}$ per cent or $\frac{1}{2}$ per cent. Generally speaking, the annual charge on UK-investing trusts is lower than that levied on trusts investing in overseas or specialised markets.

**Other Charges** In order to avoid the need for quoting unit prices for awkward fractions of a penny, the managers are entitled to make a rounding charge of both buying and selling prices of not more than 1.25p or 1 per cent, whichever is the smaller, in addition to the initial and annual charges. A further cost to the unit holder is the $\frac{1}{4}$ per cent unit trust instrument duty levied by the Government, which is included in the offer price of units.

These charges together represent the whole of the additional cost a buyer of units has to bear, compared with the investors purchasing directly on the Stock Exchange (brokerage, contract and stamp duty are payable in both cases).

**Control** Unit trusts are strictly controlled by the Department of Trade. A unit trust is set up by a trust deed, which is an agreement between the trustees and the managers of the fund. The trust deed covers the main aspects of the running of the trust and has to be approved by the DoT. The essential characteristics of the deed are that it lays down the rights and responsibilities of all concerned, the provisions enabling new members to join, the maximum charges that can be made by the managers for administrating the fund and the provision for calculating the buying and selling prices of units.

**Investment instructions** Unit trust managers are allowed only to invest in securities quoted on a recognised stock exchange, although they may also hold up to 25 per cent of their funds in companies traded on the USM of which 5 per cent may be held in unlisted securities, whether USM or not. Certain other investment constraints are included in the trust deed to ensure that each fund has a sufficiently diversified spread of risk. The most important of these constraints is that no holding may be acquired which will result, at the time of purchase, in the trust holding more than 5 per cent of its value in one investment. In practice, if an investment increases sufficiently in value after purchase it may well exceed the 5 per cent limit, but as long as its value does not exceed $7\frac{1}{2}$ per cent of the fund the trustees will not be too concerned. Another restriction on the managers is that each trust must not hold more than 10 per cent of the issued share capital of any company. But with management groups running a whole range of trusts it is not inconceivable that between their trusts they may together hold more than 10 per cent of the share capital of one particular company. Additionally, unit trusts are not permitted to invest directly in property.

The main purpose behind these constraints is to ensure that the investments held in a fund's portfolio are easily realisable. This in turn enables the managers to buy and sell units at any time.

**Buying and selling units** Units can be bought either directly from the managers or through an agent such as a stockbroker, bank, solicitor or accountant. They can also be bought through any of the offers that frequently appear in newspapers. The buying price of units offered for sale through advertisement is usually fixed until the closing date for the offer specified by the managers. Units bought after the closing date are allocated at the offer price ruling on receipt of the investor's cheque. Units in new trusts are also often offered to the public at a small discount or with a

special bonus. For example, one unit trust launched recently offered a bonus in the form of additional
units, depending on the amount invested. If units are
bought through an agent, his commission normally
comes out of the manager's initial service charge. The
UTA currently recommends that a rate of $1\frac{1}{4}$% per
cent should be paid to all agents.

Units can be sold back to the managers of the trust
by contacting the managers themselves or through an
agent. The price at which the managers will buy back
units is controlled by the DoT. No commission is paid
by the manager when units are sold back, so it could
be cheaper to sell directly to the managers rather than
through an agent.

The unit trust industry is vast, with many options
open to the investor in the form of specialised and
general investment. It is a simple and easy way to take
advantage of rising stock market prices. Competition
between the main management group of unit trusts is
fierce and their performance is closely monitored by
the financial press. Every investor with cash to spare
would be advised to put some money into unit trusts,
taking care to choose the more successful groups.

---

## 34   Is it worth buying shares in an investment trust?

Any investment trust is a limited liability company
whose shares are bought and sold through the Stock
Exchange in exactly the same way that shares are traded
in other public companies. The assets of these trusts are
shares in other listed stock market companies all
around the world. Rather like unit trusts, investment
trust portfolios are spread widely, something which the
individual acting on his own would find difficult to
achieve. When the first investment trust was formed

over 100 years ago, it had as its stated purpose 'to provide the investor of moderate means the same advantages as the large capitalists in diminishing risks . . . by spreading investment over a number of stocks'. Investment trusts are exempt from tax on capital gains realised on their portfolio of investments. This allows the investor to defer any liability to tax on capital gains until he sells his shares. In addition, investment trusts – unlike some other popular investment forms such as unit trusts – can borrow money to invest in assets, any appreciation of which benefits the ordinary shareholders. Investment trusts are not supposed to invest more than 15 per cent of their assets in any one company.

In the last couple of years the investment trust industry has undergone significant change, with the managers of trusts being required to perform more actively and successfully than in the past.

By tradition, the shares of investment trusts tend to stand in the market place at a discount to the underlying value or 'asset value' of anything up to 30 per cent. Recently the pressure on these trusts from return-conscious shareholders has led to concentration on particular and specialised fields of investment rather than on the general portfolio spreads of former times. In theory an investor can buy £10 of shares for £7 or £8 by buying investment trusts, but unless the market changes its view of that particular trust (in which case the shares will rise strongly) the investor may only get £7 or £8 for the £10 of underlying share value when he sells. Of course, one hopes that the assets themselves will have increased in value so that the investor's money will have increased.

Investment trusts can only be bought through brokers and anyone considering investing in them should consult their broker or other adviser first.

# V
# Other financial markets

**Should I put money into the money markets?**

The London money market is a vast market without any central trading floor or official regulations (beyond those imposed by the Bank of England on some of the participants like the banks and the discount houses). As its name implies, it deals in money, as opposed to dealing in stocks and shares or in commodities. In practice, money is defined as bank deposits or various short-term instruments like Treasury bills and commercial bills, which can easily be sold to raise cash or are redeemed anyway within a short period, such as 90 days.

The main users of the money markets are the professionals like the banks, who have to balance their books each day and are thus constantly buying and selling large amounts of money from the discount houses, from other banks (often through money brokers) or from large corporations, who themselves are doing the same thing. The professionals also take positions in the money markets to speculate on movements in interest rates, but normally they are simply covering their needs.

Individuals can also put money into the money markets, where the main advantage is that the interest rates paid are normally higher than those offered to small depositors by the banks. But you do need to put a fairly substantial sum in – the clearing banks will be able to do this for you but normally will not do so for less than £25,000 at a time. Money can be deposited for periods of one day (known as 'overnight money'), seven days, two weeks, three months and longer periods. Interest rates are quoted on an annual basis and paid pro-rata – i.e. if you deposit £25,000 for two weeks at 10 per cent, you will earn £96, or one twenty-sixth of the annual rate.

Treasury bills, which are issued once a week by the Government as part of its financing programme, can be bought in denominations from £5,000 upwards. They are generally issued for repayment in 91 days and pay their interest rate to the purchaser in the form of a discount on the price. These bills can be bought and sold at any time up to redemption. Local authority bonds and bills, with different maturities and different denominations are similarly available. Commercial bills (issued by companies as part of their trade financing) are available in much larger denominations, and certificates of deposit can also be dealt in from £50,000 upwards.

If you have enough spare resources or want to keep a large amount of money in liquid form for a while, then it is advantageous to use the money markets. But do consult your bank or other professional adviser, and do stick to the reputable names. Also make sure you find out what commissions or charges are being made on the lump sum – normally the banks do not charge commission but may take their turn by offering you a fraction of a percentage below the current interest rate. There are also a number of unit trusts available now with the object of investing in the money markets. Details of these can be obtained from the press or from your professional advisers. Remember that in the money markets, the return is almost always in the form of income rather than capital gain.

## What are financial futures? How can I invest in them? 36

In the autumn of 1982 the London International Financial Futures Exchange (LIFFE) began operations a stone's throw from the Stock Exchange in the Royal Exchange Building. It brought to the City some of the market opportunities available in Chicago, by allowing investors to take a view on the future movement of interest rates and currencies.

Essentially, a financial futures contract is an agreement to buy or sell a standard quantity of a specific financial instrument at a predetermined future date and at a price agreed between the parties through verbal agreements on the floor of the exchange. These contracts can then be bought and sold as the holders wish, which is broadly similar to the practice in the traded options market. There are seven contracts traded on LIFFE – a short-term Sterling deposit, a short-term Euro-market deposit, a 20-year gilt, and four currency contracts (Sterling, Swiss Franc, Deutschmark and Yen – all valued against the US dollar). This market provides facilities for large international investors such as the banks, and other financial institutions to deal around the clock, as there are already such markets operating on a different clock in Chicago and the Far East. In Britain the main investors are tending to be the large corporations, banks and investing institutions who need to hedge their exposure to interest-rate and currency fluctuations. But small investors can also participate as the amount of margin required for each contract is relatively small (see below). Dealing costs are relatively low, but small investors must know what they are doing in this expert and slightly esoteric field. If they get it right, money can be made. Most banks, stockbrokers and other financial institutions will advise individuals on how they can best deal in this market.

# The London International Financial Futures Exchange: Summary of Contracts

| Three-month Eurodollar interest rate | Three-month Sterling interest rate | Twenty-year Gilt interest rate |
|---|---|---|
| **Unit of trading** | | |
| US$1,000,000 | £250,000 | A notional stock – 20 years maturity with coupon of 12 per cent £50,000 nominal value. |
| **Contract standard** | | |
| 1. A three-month Eurodollar deposit facility arranged by the seller at one of a list of banks in London designated by the Exchange as deliverable names; or 2. A cash settlement, at the buyer's option, based on the delivery settlement price ascertained and quoted by the Exchange. | 1. A three-month Sterling deposit facility arranged by the seller at one of a list of banks in London designated by the Exchange as deliverable names; or 2. A cash settlement, at the buyer's option, based on the delivery settlement price ascertained and quoted by the Exchange. | 1. Delivery may be made of any gilt with 15–25 years to maturity. Stocks with an optional redemption date will be considered to have an outstanding term to the first redemption date. 2. Stocks must be delivered in multiples of £50,000 nominal value. 3. No variable-rate index-linked, convertible or partly-paid gilts may be delivered. 4. Stocks are not deliverable within the period of three weeks and one day before the ex-dividend date. 5. Interest must be payable half-yearly. |
| **Delivery months** | | |
| SAME FOR ALL CONTRACTS: i.e. March, June, September and December. | | |
| **Quotation** | | |
| 100.00 minus the annual rate of interest in basis points i.e. one basis point is equivalent to 0.01 per cent. | 100.00 minus the annual rate of interest in basis points i.e. one basis point is equivalent to 0.01 per cent. | Price per £100 nominal value. |
| **Minimum price movement** | | |
| One basis point i.e. 0.01 per cent (US$25) | One basis point i.e. 0.01 per cent (£6.25) | £1/32 per £100 nominal value (£15,625). |
| **Price limit\*** | | |
| 100 basis points (US$2,500) | 100 basis points (£625.00) | £2 per 100 nominal value (£1,000). |
| **Initial margin\*\*** | | |
| US$1,000, which is the equivalent of a 0.4 per cent movement in interest rates. Straddle $750. | £500 which is the equivalent of a 0.8 per cent movement in interest rates. Straddle $250. | £1,500 which is 3 per cent of contract nominal value. Straddle £250. |

**Notes:**
\*Price limits do not apply to a delivery month during the four weeks up to and including the delivery day or, for the Gilt contract, the first delivery day. No price limit applies during the last hour of each day's trading in each contract.

| FT SE 100 Share Index | US Treasury Bond | Currencies | | | |
|---|---|---|---|---|---|
| The new 100 share index, at £25 per full index point (£25,000). | US$100,000 face value notional US Treasury bond with 20 years maturity and 8 per cent coupon. | £ 25,000 | DM 125,000 | SW.FR 125,000 | YEN 12,500,000 |
| A cash settlement based on the 'Exchange Delivery Settlement Price' (E.D.S.P.) ascertained by the Exchange. | 1. Delivery may be made of any US Treasury bond maturing at least 15 years from the first delivery date in the contract month if not callable; if callable, the earliest call date must be at least 15 years from the first delivery date. 2. All bonds delivered against a contract must be of the same issue. | Currencies will be deliverable in the principal financial centres in the country of issue. | | | |
| The new 100 share index value, divided by 10; taken to 2 decimal places. | Price per $100 face value. | Price in US$ per unit of currency. | | | |
| 0.05 of a full quotation point (£12.50). | 1/32 of a point ($31.25 per contract) | 0.01 cents per £1 $2.50 | 0.01 cents per DM Equal to $12.50 | 0.01 cents per 1 SW.FR. $12.50 | 0.01 cents per 100 YEN $12.50 |
| 100 ticks (£1,250). | 64/32 ($2,000 per contract) | 5 cents | 1 cent (All equal to $1,250) | 1 cent | 1 cent |
| £1,500. Straddle £250 | $1,500 per contract | $1,000 – Same for all contracts. Straddle $375. | | | |

**On straddle positions, i.e. long and short simultaneously of different months in the same contract, where neither the contract months is 'spot', the initial margin on each pair of contracts is at the reduced rate shown.

## 37 Can I make money out of commodities?

The volume of trade in commodities has grown steadily over the years, largely due to the increase in world trade and in population. Essentially the commodities market exists to service importers and exporters of raw materials, but they also allow the private investor to take a view on the movement in prices. Historically, the first official commodity exchange was set up in 1850 in Chicago, which was the centre of the rapidly-growing American grain trade. Not long after, Liverpool established an exchange. A vital ingredient of this and all present commodity exchanges around the world is that they deal not only in the physical goods, which can be bought and sold for immediate delivery, but in futures contracts. These contracts, which form a commitment to buy or sell a certain amount of goods in a certain time, can themselves be traded on the market place. The main users of the commodity markets are producers (such as the Third World countries rich in minerals and crops), merchants (who buy and sell these commodities) and consumers (such as the manufacturing companies, who produce finished goods like cars, tinned foods and so on). One feature of commodities futures trading is the ability to trade on margin, i.e. one only has to deposit something like 10 per cent of the contract value with the broker. To take a position in these futures markets, whether for hedging purposes or for profit, usually involves opening an account with a commodity broker, who executes the order on the relevant commodity exchange. The client is normally then sent a contract detailing the quantity, delivery date, and price at which the commodity has been bought or sold. From that moment the client has an open position which – unless he wants to take possession of the physical commodity – must be closed later. If the price moves up, the client will make a profit, in which case he can sell and receive a cheque with commission deducted. If the price moves against the client, then the opening position will be showing a loss. Normally, if this opening position loss has eroded more than half of the original 10 per cent deposit, it is likely that the broker will request that either the client close the position (thus eliminating the possibility of any further loss) or that he send further funds to maintain the original 10 per cent deposit. This is known as the 'margin call'.

There are two principal commodity exchanges in London – the London Metal Exchange, in Whittington Avenue, EC3, which deals in tin, lead, zinc, copper, aluminium, nickel, silver and other materials, and the London Commodity Exchange in Mark Lane which deals in soft commodities such as sugar, coffee, cocoa, rubber, soya bean meal and so on. In addition there are markets in grain, potatoes and petroleum. But if you deal in Britain through an extablished firm of brokers you will be able to deal on many other international commodity exchanges, thereby taking advantage of wider price opportunities.

Commodity price movements can be marked, and they depend a great deal on world economic conditions and as many unpredictable factors like the weather, which can seriously affect crops, and strikes or political upheavals, which can interrupt supplies. Sometimes particular buyers enter the market to try and influence price movements. In 1982, for example, a mysterious Malaysian buyer built up his purchase of tin through London and Malaysian markets, causing the price to rise at a time when demand for tin was quite low. This operation appeared to be partly due to political action from the Malaysian government. Later it stopped and the price fell back sharply. Most major commodities are traded under the umbrella of international agreements on prices between the producing and consuming

## Commodities futures contracts

| *Exchange* | *Commodity* | *Trading months* |
|---|---|---|
| London Commodity Exchange | Sugar No.4 (Expires May 1984) | Mar/May/Aug/ Oct/Dec |
| | Sugar No.5 - White | Mar/May/Aug Oct/Dec |
| | Sugar No.6 - Raw | Mar/May/Aug Oct/Dec |
| | Coffee | Jan/Mar/May July/Sept/Nov |
| | Cocoa | Mar/May/July/ Sep/Dec |
| | Rubber | Jan/Mar/Apr/June/ July/Sept/Oct/Dec |
| | Soya Bean Meal | Feb/Apr/June/ Aug/Oct/Dec |
| London Metal Exchange | Silver | Cash – 3 months |
| | Copper Wirebars | Cash – 3 months |
| | Tin | Cash – 3 months |
| | Lead | Cash – 3 months |
| | Zinc | Cash – 3 months |
| | Aluminium | Cash – 3 months |
| | Nickel | Cash – 3 months |
| London Gold Futures | Gold | Six months forward |
| London Petroleum Exchange | Gas oil Crude | All months |
| London Grain Futures Market | Wheat and Barley | Jan/Mar/May Sep/Nov |
| London Potato Futures Market | Potatoes | Feb/Apr/May/Nov |

*Note:* Table reproduced courtesy of Inter Commodities

| Contract size | Price quoted in | Minimum price fluctuation | Minimum daily limit |
|---|---|---|---|
| 50 Metric Tonnes | £ per tonne | £0.05 | 1st 2 spot months – none. Deferred £20 from 12.30 close previous day. |
| 50 Metric Tonnes | $ per tonne | 20 cents | $40 |
| 50 Metric Tonnes | $ per tonne | 20 cents | $40 |
| 5 Metric Tonnes | £ per tonne | £1.00 | None |
| 10 Metric Tonnes | £ per tonne | £1.00 | £40 |
| 15 Metric Tonnes | £ per tonne | £1.00 | £30 |
| 100 Metric Tonnes | £ per tonne | £0.10 | £5 |
| 10,000 troy ounces | pence/troy oz | £0.10 | No limit |
| 25 Metric Tonnes | £ per tonne | £0.50 | No limit |
| 5 Metric Tonnes | £ per tonne | £1.00 | No limit |
| 25 Metric Tonnes | £ per tonne | £0.25 | No limit |
| 25 Metric Tonnes | £ per tonne | £0.25 | No limit |
| 25 Metric Tonnes | £ per tonne | £0.50 | No limit |
| 6 Metric Tonnes | £ per tonne | £1 | No limit |
| 100 fine troy oz | $ per ounce | $0.05 | No limit |
| 100 Tonnes in bulk | $ per tonne | 25c | $ 30 |
| 1,000 barrels | $ per barrel | 1c | $1 |
| 100 Metric Tonnes | £ per tonne | £0.05 | No limit |
| 40 Metric Tonnes | £ per tonne | £0.10 | £15 |

countries, but this does not always hold good when market pressures become established. If you wish to take a position in any commodity, it is worth doing a bit of research on the state of the world market in that commodity.

One important point to remember is that not only is commodity dealing a high-risk business in itself, but that there are less regulations about dealing in its field than in other financial markets. This is partly due to its international nature. The last five years have seen some quite serious crashes in the commodity market with the more ambitious small firms suffering as a result. If you wish to deal, by all means do so as long as you are aware of the risks. But do make sure the broker you use is a member of the recognised exchanges ( which are listed at the end of this book) and is not likely to abuse your position if you allow him to deal at his discretion. As with other investments you can make a lot of money in commodities but you can also lose it.

## 38   Should I become a member of Lloyd's of London?

Lloyd's of London is an insurance market in which insurance policies are placed with 21,600 individual members grouped in some 417 syndicates. Each syndicate is managed by an underwriting agent who sits at his box on the floor of Lloyd's and accepts business on behalf of his members. Each syndicate member is individually liable to the full extent of his private means for his own share of risks accepted. There are four principal markets at Lloyd's: Marine, which carries every kind of shipping and marine business; Aviation; Motors, which covers more than one in five British motorists; and Non-marine, including earthquakes, burglaries and so on. All business is brought to Lloyd's by some 272 authorised firms of Lloyd's brokers who are not restricted to dealing with Lloyd's underwriters but may place business with the large insurance companies (such as the Prudential and Commercial Union) as well.

Those wishing to become members (known as 'Names') of Lloyd's must have the support of two existing underwriting members of Lloyd's and must show that they are people of some wealth and over 21. Candidates, who may be male or female of any nationality, go before a committee for an interview and if approved their applications are considered at a full council meeting. The elected member places his or her entrance fee and lodges certain deposits with the council of Lloyd's. These are held under trust deeds, and they are sold to meet underwriting liability. Accounts at Lloyd's are run on a three yearly basis, i.e. the account for year one is not closed until the end of the third year and then only as long as profits may be released. A new member must therefore wait three years for profits on his first year's underwriting. The requirements listed below are applicable to new names elected to begin underwrits from January 1984.

### Requirements of membership of Lloyd's

| Category | Means test (£) | Deposit as per cent of premium income | Minimum Deposit (£) |
|---|---|---|---|
| Lloyd's Names | Nominal | 50 | 12,500 |
| Lloyd's Names connected and associated Names, etc. | 25,000/30,000 | 40 | 12,500 |
| | 37,500/50,000 | 35 | 14,000/17,500 |
| | 75,000 | 30 | 22,500 |

| Names resident and domiciled in the UK | 100,000/225,000 | 25 | 25,000 |
| Names resident or domiciled outside the UK | 100,000/225,000 | 35 | 35,000 |

*Note:* Premium limit not to exceed twice means show; £50,000 limit in case of Lloyd's Names with nominal means.

If you have enough resources to become a member of Lloyd's, it can provide you with a useful additional source of income. After all, you will be receiving investment income and capital appreciation from the money you have pledged to the syndicate anyway. The amount of money the syndicate will pay you from its profits will vary according to the experience and skill of the underwriter. In a good year the cheque you receive may be many thousands of pounds, in a bad year it will be less. And remember that if you are unlucky you could end up having to write a cheque to cover the syndicate loss, if major troubles emerge.

You are also technically liable for your entire possessions. However, experience over the last century has for the most part been favourable and profitable for the members – which has made Lloyd's such a large and successful insurance market.

## 39    Is it worth investing in the Euro-markets?

Eurobonds are international bonds issued by various companies and governments to raise money. Unless you are familiar with the intricacies of the bond markets it is not worth contemplating investing in them. Like other bonds, Eurobonds are issued for a specified length of time and pay a particular rate of interest.

It is a vast and largely unregulated market, and is dominated by the professional dealing houses of several countries. It does offer the investor the chance to put money into other currencies and occasionally offers opportunities not available in the domestic market (particularly the practice of issuing zero coupon bonds which offer all their returns in the form of capital gains without income) which is attractive to many investors for tax purposes. Most major firms of stockbrokers or banks in Britain should be able to advise you on how to invest in the Eurobonds market.

---

## What is the best way to buy gold? 40

Gold is extremely rare, expensive to mine, and virtually useless. Yet for over 6,000 years civilised people have fought, cheated, lied, slaved and died for it. Most of all they have hoarded it: the French kept it under mattresses, the Arabs wear it. Yet if all the 90,000 tons of gold ever mined were put together they would only form a cube measuring 19 cubic yards. About one-third of the gold mined each year goes into jewellery while official coins like South African Krugerrands, British sovereigns and Canadian maple leaves take only between 15 per cent and 20 per cent. During the 1970s the value of gold rose by 44 per cent in real terms. Such a performance could not continue. The price touched $840 an ounce at the end of 1980, but fell to $300 an ounce in June 1982. By mid-1983, however, it was back to between $400 and $450 an ounce, and in early 1985 it fell again to around $300.

For the private investor there are two sensible possibilities: gold coins and gold shares. The problem with buying gold metal in bulk, whether ingots or coins, is that it is subject to 15 per cent VAT. This you pay when buying but you do not recoup it when selling. Another disadvantage is that there is no income from dividends.

There are three popular types of coin:

**1 South African Krugerrands** These contain one ounce of pure (24-carat) gold. They are available in halves, quarters and tenths – the smaller variety make ideal presents. Krugerrands are the only truly internationally marketable gold coin and over a half of all the gold used in coins goes into them. The price is usually about three per cent higher than the market value of gold content (known as a premium). The difference between the buying and selling price is also around three per cent (end-April price = around £280).

**2 British new sovereigns** The Queen Elizabeth II sells at a small premium to the George VI. Older sovereigns fall into the rare or antique coin category, where the price is much higher than the bullion content. Sovereigns are 22-carat and contain 0.2354 of an ounce of 24-carat gold. Half sovereigns are also available. Around 13 per cent of the gold used in coins goes into sovereigns. They are fine for UK residents but are not as internationally marketable as Krugerrands. The premium over the gold content is usually around three per cent as is the difference between the buying and selling price.

**3 Canadian maple leaves** This is a fairly recent addition to the market. The maple leaf is exactly one ounce of 24-carat gold and is available in halves, quarters and tenths. It is produced by the Royal Canadian Mint from gold from Canadian mines. The premium and the buying and selling spread are both around three per cent. It is nowhere near as marketable as (1) and (2).

Most medium-sized branches of the big four UK clearing banks sell Krugerrands and sovereigns. The International Gold Corporation (the marketing arm of the South African Chamber of Mines) estimates that of the 16,000 bank branches in the UK, 11,000 sell Krugerrands – and more than 8,000 will buy them back.

Coins can also be bought in large quantities through

any of the five London bullion houses, who between them fix the price of gold twice a day (listed at the end of this book). Spink, the coins and medals specialist, also sells bullion coins. In addition it has devised a special scheme for selling sovereigns over 100 years old which are free of VAT. To avoid VAT it is necessary to hold the coins offshore: the most popular places are the Channel Islands and Luxembourg. The International Gold Corporation will supply a full list of gold dealers.

Individuals can trade gold in the futures markets, although it is more risky than either buying coins or investing in shares. The minimum contract is 100 ounces on either the American Comex Market or the London Gold Futures Market.

Gold shares have an advantage over coins in that they offer a dividend yield. But as there are no British gold mining shares, there is an additional currency risk in buying shares abroad. The most established market for gold shares is South Africa, where Anglo-American and Gold Field of South Africa dominate gold mine ownership. Australia, Canada and the USA also have gold mining shares. Here it is important to distinguish between the producing mine with proven reserves of ore, and the speculative shares from a company, most often in Canada and Australia, which may have some gold but is uncertain of the quantity and the grade.

## What is an investment diamond?                                    41

Pure crystallised carbon, close to natural graphite. More than 1400° and a pressure of 60,000 atmospheres are necessary for the molecular bonding to be diamontiferous and not graphitic. As much as 80 per cent of the world's output of gem diamonds comes from South Africa, South West Africa, the USSR and Zaire. Of all the stones produced, only between 15 per cent and 20 per cent are good enough to be used as gems. These are mainly small stones of less than one carat which most investment houses consider too small fry. Those diamonds which are more than two carats in weight are disproportionately more expensive than one carat ones, and so may take longer to put back on to the market when the investor needs to re-sell. Sizes from one or two carats are therefore considered the most suitable for investment purposes.

The principal diamond mining company is De Beers Consolidated Mines, one of the main parts of the Oppenheimer family empire. Harry Oppenheimer, son of the man who founded the company in 1917, is one of the ten richest men in the world. Companies which are either controlled by the Oppenheimers or in which they have a big stake are reckoned to account for half the value of the Johannesburg stock exchange. Harry Oppenheimer once said: 'There is no one concerned with diamonds, whether as producer, dealer, cutter or customer who does not benefit from it'. De Beers controls the supply of the bulk of uncut diamonds to world markets, though its Central Selling Organisation (CSO). This controls between 80 per cent and 85 per cent of new diamonds around the world. Those who support it claim that the CSO supplies essential stability. The investor is sheltered from violent fluctuations. If a downward trend is spotted for a certain kind of diamond, the CSO will follow a policy of holding so as to re-establish the balance between supply and demand.

You can buy diamonds from established dealers, such as those in London's Hatton Garden. The best range to choose is 1 to 1.75 carats – large enough for investment, but small enough to re-sell. Do get an independent assessment of its value on internationally accepted standards. Have an acceptable certificate, and have the diamond packaged, with it, so that there is no possibility of any dispute. Certificates come from a gemmological laboratory, like the European Gemmological Laboratory, the International Gemmological Institute and the Gemmological Institute of America. The terms of sale should include all risks insurance, if the stone is deposited in the vault of a clearing bank in the UK or the Channel Islands. A diamond is usually delivered to the place specified by the investor, with a microfilm of its certificate sealed into a transparent sachet by the organisation that has provided the certificate.

Diamond investment companies will normally only offer to re-sell a diamond on behalf of its client after two years. There will usually be a 10 per cent handling charge – you should check this. Some companies also offer a 'no loss' guarantee. This is an undertaking to resell any stones purchased from them not less than two years before at a price that, after all the handling and administration charges, enables the client to recoup the original price. The only effective means of selling your diamond is through the same diamond investment house you bought it from. So try to buy from one that is well established and highly regarded, and likely to stay in business. VAT will be payable on the purchase of a diamond unless it is taken out of the country or to the Channel Islands.

# VI
# PROPERTY

## 42   Should I invest in property?

Property – whether housing or land – is normally the
biggest investment an individual will make in his or her
life. It is also an increasingly popular investment, with
record numbers of individuals or families seeking home
ownership. As the sums involved are way beyond the
financial resources of most people, they have to borrow
money to buy the house of their choice. Building
societies account for 80 per cent of all the loans.

By and large, anyone who has invested in property
over the last twenty years will have found it a good
hedge against inflation, as house prices have for most of
the period outstripped the growth in the cost of living.
Moreover, there are significant tax advantages, in
terms of income tax relief, in borrowing money to buy a
home (the income tax relief covers the interest elements
in the repayments on the first £30,000 of a loan at the
borrower's marginal tax rate). And there is the added
advantage that when you want to sell the house, not
only is it a readily realisable asset but also the sale will
not be subject to CGT for any profit you make.

In order that the mortgage interest paid to a building
society may qualify for tax relief, the loan must be used
either for purchasing a property or for improving it or
for paying off another loan which itself was for purchase or improvement of the property. Two principal

restrictions apply:

1. The property must at the time interest is paid be the only or main residence of the borrower, his divorced or separated spouse or a dependent relative, or be so used within twelve months of the loan being made. If the property ceases to be used as the only main residence, relief may continue for a limited period (normally twelve months) in respect of a loan on that property.

2. No relief for interest is due in respect of that part of a loan which exceeds £30,000. All previous similar loans which are still outstanding must be brought into account for the purposes of this limit, but an exception is made where a borrower moves house and temporarily owns two properties for each of which there are loans outstanding.

Tax relief may also be obtained if the property is being purchased with a view to future occupation as a main residence by a borrower currently living in job-related accommodation. Interest may also qualify for tax relief where funds are raised against the security of the only or main residence of a borrower aged 65 or over and where 90 per cent or more of the proceeds of the loan are used to buy a life annuity which will end with the borrower's death or, where there are two annuitants, the death of the survivor.

---

**What are the lending policies of the building societies?**    **43**

Building societies provide loans to home-buyers who, in turn, give a mortgage to their society. The mortgage is a legal charge on the property. The mortgage deed is the legal contract between the society and borrower. It comprises: the names of the parties to the contract, i.e. the borrower and the building society; a statement of the amount of loan being made and an acknowledgement by the borrower of receipt of the loan; a promise by the borrower to repay the loan with interest on the stipulated terms; the legal charge of the property to the society until the loan is repaid; and promises by the borrower concerning insurance and repairs.

When seeking a building society loan, a prospective purchaser can use the general rule of thumb that a society will be prepared to lend $2\frac{1}{2}$ times an applicant's gross earnings. If a joint loan to two people is wanted, the multiple may be $2\frac{1}{2}$ times the gross annual income of the higher earner plus once the other income. The building society will probably want evidence of the applicant's salary from his or her employer.

While societies will lend on all types of property, provided they are structurally sound, there could be problems with:

**Properties with a short life** Most societies require the expected life of the property to be at least 30 years.

**Leasehold properties** Societies will require that the lease should run for 20-30 years after the period of the loan.

**Converted flats** Most societies will lend on converted flats as long as the conversion is structurally sound and the lease makes provision for maintenance and repair of common parts of the building.

**Freehold flats** These are not normally acceptable, because of legal difficulties over repairs.

## 44 What different types of mortgages are there?

The majority of home buyers elect to repay their mortgage loans by 'annuity loans'. These provide for regular monthly repayments such that over the life of the mortgage (normally 20 or 25 years) the debt, together with interest, is entirely repaid.

The alternative repayment method is to link a loan to

an endowment assurance plan. During the life of the loan the borrower pays interest only to his building society. Simultaneously, he pays a monthly premium to an insurance company. When the mortgage expires, the proceeds of the endowment policy are used to repay the building society loan and there could be some money left as a bonus for the home buyer. There are three types of endowment mortgages:

**A non-profit endowment mortgage** where the proceeds of the endowment policy are sufficient to repay the mortgage loan and the borrower is left with no lump sum.

**A with-profits endowment mortgage** Here the sum assured is equal to the mortgage loan but bonuses mean that the borrower receives a substantial lump sum after the loan has been repaid. The proceeds may be up to three times the amount of the loan, which has the disadvantage that it is expensive for the borrower who is participating in a savings scheme.

**A low-cost endowment mortgage** which assumes that the eventual proceeds of the policy (with bonuses) will be higher than the sum assured and so the initial sum to be assured is lower than the size of the loan. This has the advantage of reducing the premiums to be paid but you run the risk that the proceeds may not have appreciated enough to cover the loan and you will have to make up the difference.

The advantage of an endowment mortgage is that the loan will be paid off in full in the event of the borrower's death. But they have the disadvantage that when mortgage rates increase, the borrower cannot usually extend the term of his loan. Higher repayments will have to be met in full.

Whether you have an annuity mortgage or an endowment mortgage, the system by which you obtain tax relief on the interest you pay is the same. Your building society calculates the amount of basic rate tax relief you are entitled to and deducts this from your monthly mortgage repayment. So the amount you pay your building society monthly will be net of tax relief. The Inland Revenue reimburses your building society with the difference between the net figure you have paid and the figure the building society would have asked you to pay had there been no tax relief on the interest element of your repayments. This is called Mortgage Interest Relief at Source (MIRAS).

---

### 45    What costs are involved in buying a house?

In an active market, you will probably have to offer the asking price for your chosen house, but where there are plenty of houses on the market you may be able to offer less. Offers should be made 'subject to survey and contract', which means neither side is legally bound to go through with the sale at this stage. It is at this point that the building society should be formally approached for a loan. You will have to give details about the proposed house, and about your financial background to confirm that you have the ability to repay the loan. The building society will want to check the value of the property and a valuer will be called in to do that. The fee is normally calculated according to the purchase price. You are strongly advised to have a structural survey carried out; this will usually cost between £100 and £200. It may be possible to combine the building society valuation and a full structural survey with a resultant saving in costs.

The building society makes an offer of advance based on the valuation of the property or the purchase price, whichever is the lower. Normally you will only receive a portion of the purchase price from the society – around 80 per cent. The rest you will have to make up from savings. If the advance exceeds 80 per cent of the valuation, the building society will want more security. This is usually in the form of an indemnity by an insurance company for which a single premium is paid. The building society makes the arrangements and the premium is added to the loan. The loan will be unconditional, unless defects are found in the house, in which case:

1. The building society will offer the full amount of the loan on purchase but on condition that remedial work is done within a certain time limit.

2. The building society will only offer part of the loan, with the balance being paid when the necessary work is done.

You will now need a solicitor to check the mortgage deeds etc. This conveyancing of the property is an expensive business, though there is no longer a statutory scale of fees. As a rough guide, solicitors now charge a basic fee of about 1 per cent of the purchase price – e.g. £300 if the price is £30,000, and so on.

If the land on which the house is registered (and 75 per cent of houses are covered by registration), the solicitor's costs should be lower. A small charge is made for registering with the Land Registry the transfer of ownership of property.

Stamp duty, a Government tax on the purchase of houses, has to be paid where the house price exceeds £30,000. The rate charged is 1 per cent, a reduction from the 2 per cent level prevailing before the March 1984 Budget.

### 46 Is investing in a second home a good idea?

With property prices rising again, it might seem a good
idea to get into the second home market if you can
afford it. Remember, though, that raising a mortgage
on it could be difficult and when you sell it any profit
will be subject to CGT. The advantage of a second
home is that you can boost your income by letting it out
when you are not using it. The problem here is finding
trustworthy tenants. Many estate agents run special
services to help fill such homes for short lets.

### 47 Is timesharing in the UK worth thinking about?

Timesharing developments in Britain are thought to be
worth around £50 million, with some well respected
companies such as the Midland Bank, Wimpey, Bar-
ratts, SGB and Kenning involved. It started in France
in the mid-1960s and there are around 1,100 developments around the world today. In England and Wales
timesharing is restricted by the law against perpetuity,
which means that no time share unit can be sold for
longer than 80 years, nor can more than 4 people own a
freehold property. However, across the border in Scotland, and in France, Spain and many American states,
you can buy the freehold in perpetuity.

The most important point to remember, after loca-
tion (no one wants to timeshare in the Gorbals), is the
actual time of year the property will be yours. After all,
if someone was keen to sell you a month's holiday in the
Yukon in January, you would be unwise to take it.

Normally, periods of purchase are for an agreed
number of weeks, with a maximum of 12. And
remember that while it may appear to be a low-cost
holiday option, there are management costs, which will
rise with inflation or faster.

To determine who is a reputable time sharer, contact

the British Property Timeshare Association, or the Time Ownership Trade Association, a rival to the BPTA.

---

### It is worth investing in a farm? 48

It depends on how much you have to invest and how active a role you want to play. If you want to buy a farm outright, you are going to have to be in the super rich bracket. Five hundred acres, at £2,000 an acre for good quality land, is probably the minimum viable unit. On top of that a further £500 an acre will be needed for investment in livestock and machinery. People are managing to find that sort of money now – mainly those who have enjoyed the recent boom in the City. They were attracted by the boom in farming incomes in 1982 (up 45 per cent) after three years of recession. Interest has naturally pushed up the price of farming land even past that £2,000 mark (in 1982 it was £1,884 according to Strutt & Parker; see Figure1).

For the small investor, this route into farming is far too expensive and he probably will not be able to gain a tenancy either. Perhaps a dozen tenancies come onto the market each year under the Agriculture Holding Act of 1976. But there is definitely potential in farming once he can find a way in. Strutt & Parker calculate between 1945 and the present, agricultural land in England has increased in value at an average of about 10 per cent per annum, which is almost twice the increase in the Retail Price Index (see Figure 2).

The small investor's best route into farming is via some of the pension funds which have bought up farm land in recent years, attracted by the way money holds its value there. It is, however, a fairly low-yielding investment – producing a net return on book costs of about 3 to $3\frac{1}{2}$ per cent.

Property Growth Assurance offers one of the few ways into farming via its agriculture fund. Investment in the fund is through a life assurance policy, allowing tax relief on contributions and tax-free income or a lump sum after ten years. Most of the fund is invested east of the M1 motorway in good quality land. The investor puts in a minimum of £425 a year, or £42.50 monthly net, allowing 15 per cent tax relief. This money goes straight into the fund and can be used either to buy more land or for investment on existing farms to improve farming methods, crop yields and, ultimately, profits. The investor gets the benefit of the fund's growth when the life assurance policy matures after ten years. A similar, though smaller, fund is run by City of Westminster Assurance, part of the Sentry Group. And University Medical General has recently started advertising an agricultural fund claiming the time is now ripe to move into agriculture.

For those with more cash to invest, a quicker way into farming is possible through a scheme run by Agricultural Land Share Investment Limited (ALSIL), a subsidiary of the Land Improvement Group. By investing a minimum of £25,000, the individual can join a syndicate which buys a particular farm rather than investing in a general fund. The syndicate stays together for between ten and fifteen years. Four per cent of the original stake goes to ALSIL for organising the syndicate and a small annual administration charge is also levied. One advantage of this scheme, as with all investment in agriculture, is in terms of tax. Capital Transfer Tax relief of 20 per cent was increased in the 1983 budget to 30 per cent for individuals owning let land for over seven years. There are other CTT advantages in that the farmer can get 50 per cent working farmer relief or the 50 per cent business asset relief on the value of the farm at the date of transfer.

For the individual who has bought a farm, there is

100 per cent tax relief on purchasing new equipment. If he is a high income tax payer, he can run a business from his home (i.e. the farm) and offset tax against that business.

When selling a farm, there is 'roll-over relief' in respect of CGT. You do not pay CGT if the profits are invested in another business within three years.

With regard to income tax, the farmer is entitled to relief if he carries out capital improvements such as drainage. The cost of these can be written off against tax over seven years: 30 per cent in the first year and 70 per cent in the following years.

Experts reckon the outlook for agriculture in Britain is good for the forseeable future, for several reasons:
1. Because we only produce 55 per cent of our food requirements, the Government is keen to reduce the import bill. A Conservative Government normally looks favourably on the farmers' case.
2. Because industrial relations are good in farming, there is scope for improving productivity and the potential for scientific advances. The fact that agriculture is still under-capitalised also make the growth prospects extremely attractive.
3. There is a limit on the availability of land in Britain, which will put pressure on demand and so on prices. And as land values in the country are still below those of the EEC, it is reasonable to assume that we will catch up with the Europeans eventually.

Investment in farming need not be confined to Britain. There is a great deal of interest in American farm land now, in the mid-West corn belt – Indiana, Ohio and Illinois. American farming can show a return of 5 to 6 per cent and there has been an upsurge recently in the farming economy there after a couple of years of recession. Good quality land can fetch $2,000 to $3,000 an acre.

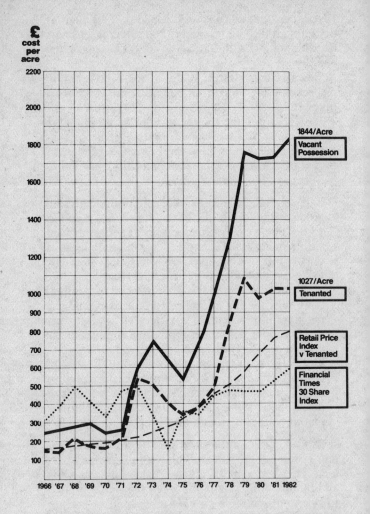

*Figure 1. The growth in agricultural land prices in England and Wales, 1966—1982*

Source: Strutt & Parker

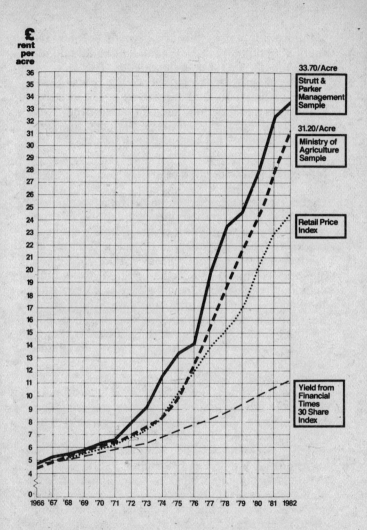

*Figure 2. The increase in agricultural rents in England, 1966-1982*

Source: Strutt & Parker

Future prosperity in Britain depends crucially on continuing support for the Common Agricultural Policy. While the CAP has been criticised – not least by British politicians – experts believe the British Government will not do anything to overturn the system.

If you are considering investing in farmland, it is generally advisable to purchase only Grade I to Grade III land (about 49 per cent of British farmland).

## 49    Is forestry a worthwhile investment?

Higher rate taxpayers have an alternative investment in farming in forestry, where there are considerable tax advantages and government grants. The Government is keen to see more forestry in Britain in order to cut down on the 90 per cent of timber we import, at present at a price of around £3 billion a year. The main difficulty in rectifying both the imbalance in imports and the potential shortage of timber in the world by the next decade is the time it takes for trees to grow. The popular Sitka Spruce, for example, takes 60 years to reach maturity and it may take 20 years for any income to appear.

To encourage initial investment, a series of tax concessions are offered. Tax on income is judged under Section D and the cost of establishing the plantation can be claimed as a business loss and set against income from other sources. Forests also count for 50 per cent business asset relief on CTT, while the appreciation in value of timber is free of CGT on disposal.

A combination of rising land and timber prices should ensure that forests increase in value faster than inflation. Specialists like the Economic Forestry Group (EFG) reckon that there could be a real annual growth rate of about $1\frac{1}{2}$ per cent in the value of forests, which can be realised either when the mature timber is sold, or if the forest is sold before maturity. Both EFG and the other major forestry group, Fountain Forestry, run large tracts of forestry for clients.

While outright purchase of, say, a 100 hectare site might cost £65,000 before planting, EFG run some 50 co-ownership trusts allowing the small investor to get into forestry investment. Each trust, with 12 to 20 members, owns some 1,000 acres of woodland managed by EFG. Individual investment varies from £10,000 to £100,000. Risks such as fire can be insured against. Disease cannot: but by diversifying into various species, this threat can be minimised.

# VII
# Small business

**50 What are the advantages of investing in small businesses?**

'Small is beautiful' is a sentiment the Conservative Government has embraced with great enthusiasm in Britain when it comes to supporting business. And many would say, not before time, too, since the small business sector in Britain is considerably smaller than in many of our more prosperous and economically more efficient competitors. Its share of manufacturing employment has risen from 27 per cent in 1973 to 30 per cent in the 1980's. However, this is still a long way behind the German figure (32 per cent), the Japanese (68 per cent) and the Americans (39 per cent).

To encourage more small business (usually defined as companies under 200 staff) in Britain, the Government has developed a range of direct and indirect aid. Today there are no less than 108 schemes (and still growing). In December 1981, there were 70 schemes. The Government has already spent £2 million on advertising to promote some of its schemes; these include the Business Expansion Scheme and the small firms' Loan Guarantee Scheme (which are discussed in detail below).

Useful as these are to the small businessman, or the potential entrepreneur, you should be wary of any red tape involved in applying for them and the sheer bewildering number of schemes. Another possible deterrent to starting or financing a small business is the recession itself. Who wants to start or back a business when markets are apparently flat and demand depressed?

The answer is, encouragingly, many, many people. From 1980 to 1982, in spite of thousands of business failures, there was actually a net increase in the number of small businesses, to the tune of 20,000.

There are failures, too. One in five of the companies backed under the Loan Guarantee Scheme goes to the wall. While institutions back what they think is a good idea (always hoping for the 100 to 1 return that some of the backers of the original high technology companies in Silicon Valley, California made), the reality can be the £1 million written off in a Norwich Union portfolio of 26 companies worth £4 million.

Most of the new small businesses are started in the South of England, according to a survey published in June 1983 by the monthly newsletter, *Venture Capital Report*. The survey of 429 projects found that 56 per cent were established in London, the South-East or the South-West. It found that the average finance required by a starting business was £139,000; there was also a heavy bias towards manufacturing, with 44 per cent, followed by the service sector with 20 per cent.

Putting money into small business, whether your own or someone else's, is definitely to be considered an attractive investment, which will receive government encouragement and perhaps financial aid and tax relief. But do not invest in small firms just for the tax relief – the business has to be a good one in its own right.

---

**If I want to start my own business, where can I get help?** 51

Finance for setting up a business comes from the following sources:

1. The personal resources of the businessman/woman.

2. Equity capital provided from outside sources or under the Business Start Up Scheme.

3. Medium and long-term finance, including leasing and hire purchase.

4. Banks.

5. Trade credit.

6. Government finance.

It is usually best to combine sources.

As we have already said, there are some 108 government schemes for helping small businesses. Full details of all of these can be obtained from the Department of Industry or any of its regional offices, but some of the schemes merit special mention here.

**The Business Start-up Scheme** was introduced in the 1981 Finance Act, and provides a tax deduction for outside (passive) investors in a new limited company, thus giving rich individuals an incentive for subscribing for shares in new companies. There is tax deduction against the general income of outside investors for their capital investment in the shares. The deduction is given regardless of the outcome. The relief is only available until 5 April 1984. Several conditions apply:

● The investment must be in the ordinary share capital of the company, either directly or through an Inland Revenue-approved fund. If the investment is direct, the minimum investment is £500 per investor, but there is no lower limit if the investment is through an approved fund.

● Relief cannot be claimed on more than 50 per cent of the company's total ordinary shares.

● The investor must live in the UK and, with certain exceptions, neither he nor his close relatives must receive fees or salary from the company, except for normal dividends.

● Relief is denied if the investor owns more than 30 per cent of the issued ordinary shares.

● The company must have started trading in a *bona fide* new venture in the last five years. It must be an independent UK-resident one, not involved in

commodity or land dealing or providing financial
services.

● The shares must be held for a minimum of three
to five years.

● The full amount invested qualifies as allowable
expenditure for CGT purposes if the shares are sold,
but any capital loss is disallowed to the extent of any
tax relief given.

This is the briefest summary of complex details; the
booklet 'Incentives for industry in the areas for expansion' issued by the Department of Industry is a useful
guide. This scheme is very tax efficient for a higher rate
taxpayer.

**The Business Expansion Scheme** Individuals can
claim tax advantages up to a maximum of £40,000
invested in small companies in any one fiscal year,
though the relief flows through only when the money is
out of the fund and is invested in the recipient company. A person paying the top rate of 75 per cent can
thus invest, say, £40,000, and it will cost £10,000 net. A
standard rate taxpayer paying £6,000 a year tax, for
example, could wipe out his tax bill by investing something like £18,000. The BES does not apply to property
and financial companies, or to companies listed on
either the Stock Exchange or the USM. The investment must be held for five years.

**The Small Engineering Firms Investment
Scheme** This was first introduced in March 1982 to
make available to engineering firms employing less
than 200 people a third of the cost of investment in
certain types of advanced capital equipment. So great
was the demand that the scheme closed for applications
in two months and the original allocation had to be
raised from £20 million to £30 million. The scheme was
re-introduced on 28 March 1983. £100 million was
allocated and almost all engineering firms employing
up to 500 people will be eligible.

**Redundancy Payments Tax Threshold** To encourage people who are unemployed, particularly those who are made redundant, to set up in business, the tax threshold for redundancy payments and other payments made on termination of employment has been raised from £10,000 to £25,000.

**Enterprise Zones** 24 of these zones have been or are being set up round the country in depressed areas. Within the zones, new and existing firms will be exempt from rates and Development Land Tax and they will enjoy 100 per cent tax allowances for capital spending on industrial and commercial buildings. Planning procedures will be greatly simplified and remaining rules speeded up.

**The Loan Guarantee Scheme** is designed to make commercial finance more readily available to small businesses which have been unsuccessful in getting finance on normal commercial terms. The Government will provide the lending bank with a guarantee for 80 per cent of the loan and the lending bank bears the risk of loss on the remaining 20 per cent. Applications can be made through a number of banks including all the main clearing banks and Investors in Industry (the newly re-named financial institution backed by the major clearing banks and the Bank of England). Applications can be made by sole traders, partnerships, co-operatives or limited companies already trading or just starting in business. Agriculture, banking and finance and public houses are among certain excluded businesses. A full list is available from any of the sponsoring bodies. The Government doubled the amount it is putting in the scheme to £600 million in the Spring 1983 budget. Guaranteed loans can be for amounts up to £75,000, repayable over periods of between two and seven years. Interest rates are determined by the lender. A 3 per cent interest rate premium is charged on the guaranteed portion of the loan to cover the cost of the guarantee. Further details from the Department of Industry's Loan Guarantee Unit, Room 212, Ashdown House, 123 Victoria Street, London SW1E 6RB (01-212 7676).

*A final point on form filling:* small businessmen frequently complain about the huge number of government forms they receive. In future government departments will be sending out three or four million fewer forms than they did in 1979. And future forms will have to be more intelligible.

---

### What help do the banks provide? 52

Banks and financial institutions can provide a 'package' of finance – small loans and share capital – which will result in the institution having a minority interest in the share capital (20 per cent to 49 per cent). They usually deal in amounts larger than £25,000. Most of the clearing banks and their merchant banking arms now have divisions dealing with this. Investors in Industry have a long record of providing this kind of finance.

---

### Do I have to go just to the Government or to the banks if I want help? 53

No. British venture capitalists are coming forward all the time. The term 'venture capital' was coined in the USA and refers to the original backers of the high technology companies in Silicon Valley, California. Around £300 million worth of venture capital money is now available in Britain for investment each year. Around two-thirds of the venture capitalists are in the British Venture Capital Association, representing 33 of the major companies in the field.

If it is advice or other help you need beside finance,

there are a plethora of schemes available. For example, the Abbey National, with the Industrial Society and Capital Radio, offers a year's free office accommodation to young entrepreneurs in a Head Start for Business campaign. The Industrial Society offers unlimited use of its information service to companies with under 50 staff for an annual fee of £50. Similarly, the London Enterprise Agency provides advice in the fields of property, finance, marketing and innovation. The National Federation of the Self-Employed and Small Businesses covers all its 50,000 members with an insurance policy guaranteeing £1,500 worth of professional advice, if their affairs are subject to in depth investigation by the Inland Revenue.

There is also the Government's Small Firms Service – an information system which was established in 1972 solely for owners or prospective owners of small businesses. It has expanded dramatically since then: in 1982 they received nearly double the number of enquiries received in 1981.

---

**54    If I want to start my own business, what are the pitfalls to avoid?**

The first point you must remember is that although it is a daunting prospect to leave the shelter of a salaried position within a large organisation, the rewards of running your own business and being the boss can be immense and not simply in financial terms. Job satisfaction is normally much higher (helped by the fact that a successful entrepreneur can quite literally make an eventual fortune by floating his company on the stock market).

That said, there are a lot of risks. First, small businesses must be run on a sound financial footing. Many apparently excellent firms with splendid products go to the wall because they have over-extended themselves. This can be overcome to some extent by bringing in outside expertise, and if you go to venture capitalists for support they will adopt a 'hands-on' approach, i.e. they will put management as well as money into the company. Remember always to shop around in the venture capital field if you have a good idea, since the days have long gone when British entrepreneurs were starved of resources. While the venture capitalist will charge a higher rate of interest on a loan or demand a stake in the company (which is fair enough, as you are by the nature of things a high risk investment until you have a track record), you can get different terms by asking around in the venture capital market, such as lower loan terms of a smaller stake demanded in your company. And while you will have to work much harder than you ever did in the past, the incentive will be simply that you have probably had to commit everything you have to the venture, including your house. This is quite normal. Why should an entrepreneur expect anyone to back his business if he is not prepared to do so himself? It is an excellent motivator.

In running your own business, you will need a clear idea of what you are trying to do when, how much it will cost, the market share you hope to achieve; in other words, a complete business plan. It's no good just having a few bright ideas and a Double First in Genetic Engineering from Cambridge, without having a clear idea of how your biotechnology company is going to operate. Help in working out a business plan will always be given by a venture capitalist or any other potential source of support.

## Can I invest in small businesses through a managed fund?     55

Yes. The traditional route is via one of the specialist unit trusts that look for good small companies to invest in, ones normally quoted on a stock exchange. There are a number of these. M & G have the Smaller Companies Fund and the American Smaller Companies Fund. Save & Prosper have the Smaller Companies Income Fund, and there are many more. Advice on which to join should be obtained from your broker. In the summer of 1983 a number of funds aimed at exploiting tax relief under the Business Expansion Scheme were launched, and have proved quite popular.

The BES has opened up a whole range of new opportunities for the private investor who wants to get into small businesses. Taking advantage of the tax relief proposals with investments in unquoted companies, City institutions are now offering a range of funds. For example, Granville and Co. has the Granville Business Expansion Fund, while Lazards and Development Capital Group are also linked in a similar fund. Laurence Prust (who launched the very successful Basildon Fund doing similar work) joined with Oakland Management Investment to launch the £3 million Alpha Business Expansion Fund. And there have been many more since then.

Aside from these funds, if you want to invest direct into a small business, one way is via the USM. But, as we have said earlier, it is usually an expensive investment unless you can get the shares in the original placing.

If you are wondering whether to become a venture capitalist on your own, the simple answer is don't. It is expensive, very risky and requires a great deal of expertise. However, those venture capital companies in the USA who go for a 'hands-on' approach and wait for up to ten years to reap the rewards of their investment are normally hoping that they will recoup ten times their original stake, which is a very good rate of return indeed.

# VIII
# PUTTING MONEY ABROAD

**What are the first things to consider?** 56

Since the relaxation of exchange controls in 1979, investing abroad to make money has become a feasible option for the investor. But that said, remember:

1. Many other countries may not have similar policies and it could be difficult to remit your money back to the UK. In general, the Third World authoritarian regimes are particularly strict on this score.

2. Political stability, which we take for granted in the UK and which underpins economic prosperity, is often rare. A volatile country makes for nervous investors. Your investments are liable to nationalisation or destruction at the whims of a regime operating outside the normal rules of commerce.

3. Information about the country, its economy and price sensitive information may not get to you quickly enough for you to react, or language problems might intervene.

But bearing that in mind and assuming you take professional advice, be it from a British broker with a good reputation for overseas expertise (see below) or a bank or overseas broker with an office in London, do not forget that many overseas markets have done very well in the past. Japan and the other sunrise economies of the Far East (Singapore, Hong Kong, Korea) stand out here. Growth rates of 8 to 10 per cent a year have been commonplace and though the figure may not match that now, it is certainly a lot higher than the British rate.

---

**57 When travelling abroad, is it best to buy currency before I go?**

It depends on the country. You will get a better rate by buying the 'strong' or 'hard' currencies in Britain before you go overseas. This is because the hard currencies (at present the US dollar, the Deutschmark, the Swiss and French francs and Dutch gilders) are sought-after in the UK, whereas Sterling is less desirable in the hard currency countries. So British banks will give you a better rate. The reverse is true of the 'soft' or 'weaker' currencies (which currently include the Belgian franc, the Spanish peseta, the Portugese escudo and the Italian lira). These are better bought when you arrive at your foreign destination, where the banks or financial institutions will be more glad to get their hands on Sterling than British banks are to be given the weak currency.

When actually changing the money, the best place to do it, whether in Britain or abroad, is always at a bank. The hotel or *bureau de change* charge a bigger fee and you will get a worse exchange rate.

When going abroad with travellers' cheques it is always preferable to take the local currency. This should ensure that you pay the one per cent commission for travellers' cheques only once and you will not have to pay again to change them.

---

**58 Can I make money by speculating in foreign currencies?**

Yes – but it is a nerve-racking and very fast-moving business best left to the professionals. If you sell currency at a profit as a UK resident, you will pay CGT subject to the annual exemption prevailing at the time. This rule applies unless you can prove to the Inland Revenue that the profit arose on an account held in a foreign currency to service a commitment in that currency – to pay foreign rents or taxes for example. The Inland Revenue is hardly going to accept that a fixed-term deposit account in a foreign currency was held for such a reason. If you sell currency at a profit whilst not resident, you will not have to pay CGT. This is, of course, subject to the 36-month rule – the necessary period of non-residence before capital gains during tax year of return to UK become non-liable to tax.

You can open a foreign currency bank account in a British bank, or in a foreign bank, but it must be declared to the Inland Revenue. You can speculate on currency markets through the financial futures market (see Question 36).

## Should I buy property overseas? 59

Only if you do it through a reputable British agent with impeccable overseas connection. There are a lot of unscrupulous people in the field and the property laws vary widely between countries. Do not forget that currency movements can wipe out any capital gains.

Spain has been considered a cheap investment at certain times. Anything over £20,000 may be worth. buying, but it must be in a prime site, near a leisure complex. Villas on the Costa del Sol with three to four bedrooms and swimming pool are naturally much more expensive – fetching £150,000 or over.

The American property market can also offer good opportunities. But again, check with a reputable agent.

### 60    Is it easy to transfer money abroad?

Any bank can do it for you through an international money transfer or an express international money transfer (via a telex) in both Sterling and foreign currency. Another way to do it is to buy a bankers' draft and remit it to a third party or your own account, and the bank overseas holding your account will pay up when you show proof of your identity. The charges for this service are reasonable. The money order or draft normally costs £2.50 for every £1,000 sent abroad. The minimum charge is £3 and the maximum irrespective of the sum is £30.

### 61    Can I open a foreign currency bank account?

Yes, you can do it at any British bank – both as a current and as a deposit account. The charge for this may vary from bank to bank and may be more than that involved in an ordinary Sterling account. You can also open accounts at foreign banks, which will involve charges and procedures according to that institution's domestic laws. Such accounts must be declared on your tax return. For those travelling regularly abroad or investing overseas, having a foreign currency account can be helpful – but currency movements can be highly volatile, so you need to be aware of the risks.

### 62    Can I invest in overseas stock markets?

Yes. Although the London Stock Exchange, along with the American and Japanese markets, is one of the most important in the world, there are opportunities for the British investor to cash in on better growth rates or higher profitability of foreign companies on overseas exchanges. As a general rule, when investing on a foreign exchange it is important to take into account not just the share price but crucially the currency and interest rates. Any gain in a share price can be quickly wiped out by currency movements.

Investing overseas has its particular advantages. First, there are special situations of which you can take advantage and which you do not get in the UK often. For instance, French champagne companies are always worth considering in a good year for champagne. Second, yields are normally better overseas than in the UK. Third, by going overseas it is possible to move into countries in different parts of the economic cycle at different times. So you should be able to keep your investments in recovery or booming stocks and get out when you think the market has peaked.

There are, of course, disadvantages. First, the market hours may be limited to a couple a day (this is especially true in Europe), though this can be somewhat overcome by after-hours dealings through brokers. Second, there are some extremely 'heavy' stocks with prices that are way beyond the reach of the average investor. One Swiss drug company recently had a full share with a value of £26,500, though there were one-tenth shares at only £2,500. Third, the cost of dealing in Europe might put some private investors off. There could be a double commission to the British broker and to an overseas broker as well.

Delivery and settlement is now far smoother than it used to be, though the Spanish and Italian markets are still far from satisfactory and experts advise giving them a miss. It could take a week to get all the documentation to those countries and often the only way to do it is to hand deliver when on holiday. In addition, Italy has stringent rules whereby the investor has to put cash up front before dealing in the market.

**Germany** This is the fourth largest in the world after

the UK, Japan and the USA. It is not any bigger than this simply because much of German industry is in private hands and also because the eight German stock exchanges have a much more limited role than London in financing the corporate sector. Only 0.5 per cent of total company financing comes through issuing shares (the main source of money being the banks). Turnover on the German exchanges is low because holdings are concentrated and major shareholders are not in shares for a quick profit. Germany has not been very rewarding lately to investors. In 1980–81 the squeeze on corporate profits was the most severe since the Second World War, with a real decline of 25 per cent in 1980 and again in 1981. But Germany now has potential because as a trading nation it will always benefit from any upturn in world activity.

**Switzerland** has few restrictions on foreign investors and free trade. This makes it attractive for foreign investors. But as in Germany, it is the long-term investor who is most commonly found.

**France's** stock market has suffered far less under a socialist regime than was originally feared, though the market has reacted badly to some of the austerity measures announced by the Mitterand Government. The French market actually received a boost with tax concessions for domestic investors (the *Loi Monory*). These added some 800,000 participants to the equity market. On top of that, nationalisation has reduced the number of shares for investors to chase, which is likely to push up prices or hinder the creation of an active market.

**The Netherlands,** though large for the size of the economy, has had a diminishing number of listed companies (down by 200 in ten years). Why? Because Dutch companies prefer to raise money via private loans from the financial institutions. International companies actually outnumber domestic ones in the listings of the Dutch market.

**Scandinavia** has been an active market lately. The Stockholm market was among the world's top performers in the early 1980's because of foreign capital pouring into the country, tax relief and share savings schemes. Foreign investment in Sweden is restricted by regulations governing the purchase of Swedish shares by non-residents. Norway, by contrast, finally abolished restrictions on UK investors in the Spring of 1982.

**The USA** Here there are no exchange controls and the market is huge. The British investor should note the different types of market. At the top is the prestigious New York Stock Exchange (NYSE), dealing in about 1,700 stocks, such as IBM, General Motors, etc. Then there is the American Stock Exchange dealing in stock which is not quite as active as on the NYSE. A computerised national market also exists; this is known as the Over the Counter Market, dealing in perfectly respectable shares. And many stocks can be traded on the floor of regional stock exchanges also – such as the Kansas City Exchange and the West Coast Exchange.

Charges in America for dealing have been negotiated since 1975 when fixed commissions were abolished. Provided the investor knows which share he wants, he can save himself the expense of supporting a costly research effort by dealing through an 'execution boutique'.

Although America is far the biggest equity market in the world (and in the one year from August 1982 the value of American stocks and shares rose by a staggering $800 billion). British investors should not forget US disclosure laws. Depending on the percentage of shares held, ownership will have to be declared. Federal laws require disclosure if 10 per cent of a company's shares are held, though some states require disclosure for as little as one per cent.

**Japan** The Tokyo equity market is dominated by the

'Big Four' securities houses – Nomura, Daiwa, Nikko and Yamaichi – which together account for around half the trading volume. Nomura is by far the largest, accounting for nearly a fifth of trading volume on the Tokyo Stock Exchange itself. All the Big Four have London offices offering research in dealing facilities for private investors in the UK. Nomura in London, for example, offers regular seminars and portfolio planning, organises trips to Japan for its clients and a comprehensive list of publications and a telephone advisory service to help clients keep in contact with Japan.

**Hong Kong** This is regarded as a very volatile market, despite the recent agreement between Chinese and British Governments on the colony's future. But a good dealing profit can be made.

For investors wanting to get into Europe certain brokers like James Capel are particularly strong in the field. Alternatively, the unit trusts in Europe include GT European, London & Brussels, S & P European, Henderson European, M & G European, Schroder Europe, Hill Samuel European, Murray-Johnstone European, and Stockholder European. Brokers with a strong Japanese interest include Phillips & Drew and Vickers da Costa. You will probably need to put up £6,000–£7,000 to invest directly in Japan. American brokers with a strong British presence include Merrill Lynch and Salomon Brothers.

---

### 63  Is it advantageous, tax-wise, to work overseas?

In general, British citizens who move overseas for relatively short-term contracts (two years, for example, in the Middle East) can save a great deal of money. Usually the jobs they go to are advertised as tax-free and this is where the savings are made. But there are a number of pitfalls to watch out for. Anyone who leaves the UK solely to work abroad should apply to the Inland Revenue to be regarded as not resident from the day after his departure to the day prior to his permanent return to resume residence. The expatriate is regarded as non-resident for the duration of an overseas contract if:

1. the period of expatriation encompasses at least one full UK tax year (6 April to 5 April following) and

2. all the duties of the overseas employment are performed abroad and

3. visits for whatever reason back to the UK are limited to less than 183 days in any one tax year.

Having a home in the UK does not invalidate non-resident status, provided you have not retained part of the dwelling for your use during visits. Leasing the home to tenants prevents it being available to you. But the rents from letting UK property are regarded as 'UK source income' and thus are assessable for income tax. The dividends from UK-based companies will continue to be subject to tax. Should your investments be companies outside the UK, dividends will not be subject to UK tax whilst you are non-resident. However, some of the overseas investments may be taxed in the country in which the income arises, so watch out for the effect of any Double Taxation Agreements, which vary from country to country. You may consider re-investing to minimise or eliminate the payment of taxes. Any bank will help you and give advice on this matter.

**If I don't wish to sell an asset before I return home, how can I reduce my CGT commitment?** **64**

The first rule to remember about CGT is that the higher the acquisition value, the less any potential CGT assessment will be. For such assets as shares and unit trusts, 'bed and breakfasting' is a legal and often viable tax avoidance ploy. By arrangement with your broker or banker assets are sold at the end of one day's trading and re-acquired at the beginning of the next – hence 'bed and breakfasting'. Provided such an exercise is carried out whilst you are non-resident, you will avoid CGT and a higher acquisition value is established for future CGT purposes.

# IX
# Art, antiques and others

**When is the best time to buy art and antiques?** 65

The art and antiques market had a bad time in the years
1980–2, like most alternative investments. This has
been reflected in falling profits and cuts in staff rolls at
some of the more prestigious auction houses like
Sotheby's. But, by mid-1983, with a return of the
Conservative Government, a Stock Market boom,
economic recovery and a weak pound, the market
picked up. A number of German buyers have been
noticed at British sales, taking advantage of the cheap
pound. At the time of writing, the market in London
looked quite strong, and it is contributing well over £50
million to Britain's invisible trade balance. However,
like in other markets, sentiment can change rapidly, so
a prospective buyer or seller has to keep an eye on
prices and trends. But in the longer term, prices of
quality items tend to rise, so short-term timing is less
crucial.

**How do I choose what to buy?** 66

Always buy the best you can afford; quality rather than
quantity. And always buy what you like. Even those
who profess to have no interest in collecting or
appreciating art and its offshoots will often find that
when they are guided towards a possibly good investment they will actually not be able to bear the idea of

having it in the house, so a process of elimination occurs.

Areas which have suffered and where the market has collapsed are those which were used mainly for investment and were subject to the same volatility as the stock market. Collectors, on the other hand, keep on buying as long as they can afford it, so these goods have a longer-term price stability.

---

### 67   Is it best to make a collection?

A collection will always fetch a better price than a number of totally unrelated pieces. You can collect anything; make it an interesting and coherent collection that catches your interest and it will, perhaps, catch the interest of a buyer when you wish to sell.

---

### 68   Is attribution important?

It makes a lot of difference to the investor. The danger of course is that after a few years, a work of art may be downgraded and become classified only as 'thought to be by . . .' or 'School of . . .' To be mercenary, the only valuable thing about a work of art is who it's by. Some well-known forgers, however, are eminently collectable, but that's for interest value rather than anything else.

---

### 69   Where do I go for advice?

It is important to read up as much as possible yourself before venturing into the field. Once you have decided on ancient Brazilian teapots, subscribe to the *Ancient*

*Brazilian Teapot Monthly;* a list of relevant publications
will be available at your local library who will also order
for you any books that you need. Otherwise, go to one
of the auction houses, to their resident expert, who is
dying for the opportunity to discuss one of his pet
subjects and will love telling you all about the said
teapots. Your local antique shop may be helpful,
although it is a good idea to do your homework first. Is
it a member of one of the three main trade associations –
The British Antique Dealers' Association, the London
and Provincial Antique Dealers' Association, and the
Society of Fine Art Auctioneers? If it is, then this
suggests that the owner has some sort of good reputation. If the dealer is friendly and interested, cultivate
him. He will be able to look out for pieces for your
collection, advise you about authenticity, and generally
help you with advice.

Contact another collector, if you can.

---

**Are auction houses better than dealers?** 70

They have less of an axe to grind. They do not own the
pieces, and are interested in maintaining their reputation, and earning their commission. They too can make
mistakes, but it is in their interests to be scrupulously
honest. There are guarantees on certain things. If you
can prove within a specified period – something like
five years, but it varies – that the catalogue description
of an object is wrong, then you will get your money
back. Remember though, that there is a complex grad-
ing of attribution that affects the value. If it says
'thought to be by', or 'school of', then you do not have
much of a leg to stand on. If it states categorically that it
is a Canaletto, and you can prove beyond reasonable
doubt, backed by expert opinion, scholarship, scientific tests, that it is not, then you are covered.

**71    How does an auction house work for me if I want to buy or sell?**

There are two ways the auction house will be notified of prospective vendors. First, the private vendor can bring a sales item to one of the auction house branches scattered around the country (Phillips has thirteen) or alternatively the auction house is approached by both professionals and private individuals (such as solicitors, executors or estate agents) and can give a whole range of advice on taxation, investments, probate, house sales, valuations, and the best way to sell an item and realise an asset. The auction house will then send a valuer to see the prospective vendor and he will give a verbal valuation for an item to be sold or a written valuation for insurance probate.

The auction house arranges for the carriage and insurance of goods to its premises, where they are directed to the relevant specialist department and meet up with the goods brought in by the private vendor. The items are examined and valued by specialists, photographed, and selected for a suitable sale. This may be just an ordinary sale or it can be a highly important sale. Recently, for example, a sale at Sotheby's of Impressionist and Modern Paintings beat all previous records, when £23.2 million was raised.

Items are allocated a lot number and described in the sale catalogue. It is now the turn for pre-sale publicity to swing into action. Advertisements and press releases are sent out to all the relevant papers or magazines. Catalogues are sent to all relevant subscribers, dealers, museums or libraries. Viewing can be arranged before the sale and sealed bids will be accepted from those who cannot attend in person.

After the sale itself, the vendor should receive payment within two or three weeks outside London, and a week from London sale rooms.

## Commissions charged at the main auction houses

*Bonhams*
Buyers 10%
Sellers: private 12%
              10% after £500
Trade 6%

*Christie's*
Buyers 8%
Sellers 10%
South Kensington: 15% to seller only

*Phillips*
Buyers 10%
Sellers: 12½% up to £500
      10% over £500

*Sotheby's*
Buyers 10%
Sellers: private 15% up to £500
              10% over
Trade: 10% up to £500
      6% over

---

**Where do I keep the pieces once I have bought them?**    72

That depends how big they are, for one thing. Bear in mind that if you live in a modern bungalow, with modest-sized rooms, antique French furniture or large canvases are impractical, to say the least. If they are very good examples, then museums may be happy to take them on loan, which is useful as they will undertake the cost of keeping and insuring them.

It also depends on how replaceable they are, and what conditions are best for keeping them. For example, some of the Impressionists painted on wood, and if you hang such a painting above a radiator then its life will be considerably shortened, your investment will go up in smoke, and you will have ruined a beautiful object. French furniture is seriously affected by central heating, too. If you have a large house, with room for a gallery, or rooms that a large enough to keep objects in them, without heating and with care, then fine. If not, think about collecting glass, or silver, or other more manageable things. If the items are delicate, keep them out of reach in a glass-fronted cabinet. If you don't trust the children or the dog, don't buy them, or keep them in a safe or in the bank. If they are irreplaceable, because of their rarity or their sentimental value, it would be foolish not to keep them in the bank. Jewellery, for example, can either be copied in paste for wearing, or can be taken out and worn on special occasions.

### 73 What about insurance?

In every case, and particularly if the objects are very valuable and/or portable, insurance is vital. *Check your household insurance.* It is often woefully inadequate. Most insurance companies give no cover unless there is adequate security. Some insist on a wall safe. Others will not have anything to do with you unless you keep your valuables in a bank vault. Others specify a burglar alarm as well, linked to the police station. If you have already spent a substantial sum on buying it, it is ridiculous not to spend the extra few per cent on keeping it safe. Don't expose your property to risk: take a lesson from the experts. Protecting its valuables is one of the reasons why the art world is so secretive.

### 74 How do I find out how much a piece is worth?

If you have been keeping an eye on prices, and think that the time has come to realise your investment, take it along to your friendly dealer/expert/auction house. All three will be on the ball. The auction house will charge nothing for a verbal valuation, but it will only be rough. If you want a written valuation, either for interest or tax or probate purposes, which they will stick to, it will probably cost $1\frac{1}{2}$ per cent of the price up to £10,000, 1 per cent from £10,000 to £100,000 and $\frac{1}{2}$ per cent after that. If the piece is too big, then bring in a photograph. If it looks interesting, an expert will come and have a look at it if you pay his expenses.

If you want to sell something very rare, and you are among the three people in the country collecting your Brazilian teapots, go to one of the auction houses. If they think they can sell them, they will accept the pieces on a reserve basis. This means that a figure is agreed, below which you will not go. If the pieces do not fetch this price, they will be withdrawn. Commission will still be charged, unless you put them back in on a different date for less money, or unless you are a very good customer, in which case the auction house just would not have the nerve to ask you for the money.

---

**Are rare books a worthwhile investment?** 75

Yes. After a worldwide recession in 1981–2, the market is holding up now. As one Christie's expert put it recently; 'Following the trend of recent years, some outstanding prices were realised for exceptional items which offset the lower volume of sales of both printed books and manuscripts in the 1982–3 season. The market remained steady for anything less than superb, but showed astonishing buoyancy when its appetite was whetted.'

For the future, plate books (botanical and topographical) and modern first editions are considered worth investing in, and for under £500 investors should go for signed limited editions of early literature. Some of Christie's sales have demonstrated the strength of the natural history market. Brookshaw's *Pomona Britannica* (1812) made £26,000, and a subscriber's copy of Lear, *Illustrations of the Family of Psittacidae or Parrots* (1832) went for £22,000. Political material is also climbing in value. One unpublished autographed letter by Marx accompanied by a letter from his son-in-law went for £5,508 recently.

Rare books should therefore continue to climb usefully in value. With careful selection the investor can continue to make the 18 per cent compound annual return that rare book collecting made in 1980. Anything rare and unusual will always find willing purchasers.

## 76 What are the best hedges against inflation?

A survey by experts at Phillips produced the following results:

|  | Items which should continue to be a hedge against inflation |
|---|---|
| Furniture | **Under £500:** Edwardian; marquetry furniture.<br>**£500–£3500:** good Victorian, Edwardian; marquetry.<br>**Above £3500:** 18C writing furniture & chair sets. |
| Paintings watercolours, prints. | **Under £500:** good English drawings 1750-1820. Modern British watercolours.<br>**£500–£3500:** best watercolour artists. Topographical & sporting prints.<br>**Above £3500:** best 18C English drawings, watercolours. Good Old Master drawings. |
| Objects of art, clocks, watches, etc. | **Under £500:** Bronzes. Modern wrist watches.<br>**£500–£3500:** Napoleonic prisoner work. 17C & 18C European. |
| Carpets and rugs, etc. | **Under £500:** Turkoman bags; small nomadic rugs.<br>**Above £3500:** quality antique. |

| | |
|---|---|
| Ceramics and glass | **Under £500:** 18C English porcelain figures & tea wares.<br>**£500–£3500:** finely painted 19C cabinet pieces. Good services. French paperweights.<br>**Above £3500:** early, quality & best condition items from major 18C factories. |
| Silver, gold and plate | **Under £500:** wine labels, spoons. Small items.<br>**£500–£3500:** early spoons. Flatware services. Good Victorian silver. Omar Ramsden.<br>**Above £3500:** George I & Queen Anne silver by good makers. Gold snuff boxes. |
| Jewellery | **Under £500:** attractive, small jewellery, antique & Edwardian.<br>**£500–£3500:** signed jewellery by Cartier, Boucheron, Fabergé etc.<br>**Above £3500:** coloured diamonds, oriental pearls. |
| Art nouveau and deco | **Under £500:** cameo glass of lesser factories.<br>**£500–£3500:** jewellery. |
| Oriental | **Under £500:** 19C blue & white. Hardstone snuff bottles.<br>**£500–£3500:** Lacquer. K'ang Hsi famille-verte. Ming celadon.<br>**Above £3500:** 17C, 18C porcelain. |
| Books | **Under £500:** fine bindings. Signed limited editions of good literature. Plate books. |
| Other specialised subjects & collectors' items | **Under £500:** samplers. Edwardian miniatures. Quality postcards.<br>**£500–£3500:** 17C miniatures. 18-19C firearms, edged weapons.<br>**Above £3500:** fine European arms & armour. |
| Postage stamps, etc. | 19C issues of most countries; rare items: in all price ranges. |

## What are the best bets outside furniture and paintings? 77

A survey of antiques (not included in the main stream furniture and painting categories) by 130 specialists at Phillips around the UK, Europe and North America highlighted the possible winners in 1984/85. See tables overleaf.

|  | Items strongest in demand in 1984 |
| --- | --- |
| **FURNITURE** | Fine English period. Sets of chairs, pedestal dining tables. Decorative period furniture such as lacquer, Regency; giltwood & gesso mirrors. Inlaid Edwardian, good Victorian. |
| **PAINTINGS** | Australian and topographical. Orientalist. Modern British. |
| **WATER-COLOURS** | Mid-Victorian. Bird pictures by Thorburn etc. Scottish colourists. |
| **PRINTS** | 18C colour mezzotints & stipple engravings in period frames. Good topography. Rembrandt etchings. Prints by major modern masters. |
| **CLOCKS OBJECTS OF ART etc.** | Good longcase & small bracket clocks. 18C tea caddies. 18, 19C ivory figures. Mother-of-pearl, tortoiseshell. |
| **CARPETS, RUGS etc.** | Large, decorative, Mahal, Ziegler, Heriz. |
| **SILVER AND PLATE etc.** | Good Victorian. Good Italian, French & German. Quality modern. Small collector items. |

| For 1984 Buyers – items considered 'underpriced' | Specialists' recommendations in 1985 |
| --- | --- |
| Run-of-mill 'brown' furniture, particularly large. size. Gordon Russel & hand-made 1900-1920 period. County chairs in pairs or more. Oak | **Under £500:** George II drop leaf dining tables. **£500-£3000:** Early George III mahogany bureaux, kneehole desks and chests. **Above £3000:** Period lacquer, gilt, marquetry. |
| 18 & 19C landscapes. Post-1960s British: Frink, Piper, Sandra Blow, Lowndes, Tunnard and Proctor. | **£500-£3000:** Modern British. **Above £3000:** English landscapes **Above 10000:** Examples of British artists' best works |
| Good marine watercolours. Late 18C English portraits, especially in pastel. | **Under £500:** Good quality, 2nd echelon Victorian; fine quality portraits. **to £3000 & above:** Late 18 and early 19C English. |
| Black & white mezzotint portraits. British prints in general. Minor masters. | **Under £50:** Black & white modern British etchings. **£50-1000:** Almost all good British prints. |
| Carriage & Victorian bracket clocks, c. 1850. 19C & earlier metalware. Scrimshaw, straw-work | **Under £1000:** Gold watches. Good 19C French carriage clocks. **Above £3000:** Longcase marquetry. Prisoner-of-war items. |
| Run-of-mill Turkoman. Turn of century mid-quality Caucasus. | **Under £500:** 20C Turkoman, Belouchi rugs. **£500-3000:** Medium Kashans, good Caucasus 'collector' quality rugs. |
| 1870s/80s English silver. Scottish provincial silver. | **Under £500:** Good electroplate, Old Sheffield. **£500-£3000:** Sauceboats, coasters, coffe & tea services, inkstands. **Over £3000:** Soup tureens, centrepieces; Paul Storr. |

| | |
|---|---|
| **JEWELLERY** | Art Deco, Edwardian. Signed (Cartier, Boucheron etc.) Fine rubies & sapphires. Earrings, necklaces, rings – and tiaras! |
| **CERAMICS AND GLASS ORIENTAL** | High quality English & French porcelain. Royal Worcester, Derby, Meissen. 18C English English Majolica ware. |
| **ORIENTAL** | 18C Chinese export porcelain. 19C Canton blue & white. Late silver-mounted cloisonné. Japanese lacquer. |
| **ART NOUVEAU AND DECO** | Items of good quality and by highly regarded names. Doulton, Martinware, Moorcroft. |
| **OTHER SPECIALISED SUBJECTS & COLLECTORS' ITEMS** | Rare Victorian photographs. Natural history books, MSS. Japanese arms, armour. Embroidered pictures, samplers. Tinplate toys, soldiers. French, German dolls; teddy bears. Gold items. |
| **POSTAGE STAMPS** | Classic European and GB, especially the very quality are highlighted and most countries |

**Market Choice for 1985**

Irrespective of their specialisation, Phillips specialists were asked to name items in the saleroom market they consider the best 'buys' likely to appreciate in value.

For the first time since 1977 furniture is ousted from its No 1 position. The strongest support comes for aspects of the picture market – with **watercolours** overwhelmingly the most popular choice. It reflects the market strength in good quality Victorian watercolours. Modern British paintings are also favoured.

| | |
|---|---|
| Natural pearls, tiepins, Victorian brooches, gold items. | **Under £500:** Victorian. Swiss enamels & cameos. **£500-£300:** Georgian earrings. Edwardian; art nouveau & deco. **Above £3000:** Fine coloured stones. Cartier 1900-35. Diamond earrings. Fabergé. |
| 18C drinking glasses & early 19C glass ware. | **Under £500:** Dessert services, Victorian tea sets, English polychrome. Delftware. Georgian glass. **To £3000:** Derby porcelain figures. |
| Small, quality jade carvings. Turn-of-century Japanese prints. | **Under £500:** Ming Celadon, snuff bottles, cloisonné. **To £3000:** K'ang Hsi blue & white. Bronzes. |
| Furniture & sculpture by other than well known names. | **Under £500:** Furniture; Doulton faience; some silver. **To £300:** Carpets. **Above £3000:** Carpets by names such as Morris, Voysey etc. |
| Framed antique maps. Eastern mail armour. New Guinea artefacts. 18C fans. Early wax dolls. Early 20C golf clubs. | **Under £500:** Golf ceramics. Dinky toys. Tibetan tri-gugs. **To £300:** Natural history & travel books. Cased pistols. Oriental textiles. Rare Britains toy soldiers. **Above £3000:** Early atlases. Maori figures. Fine swords. |

rare, have done well. In most areas and price ranges, the best have areas with scope for growth.

**Furniture**, however, continues to remain strong as second choice, with the accent on top quality English of the 18th century. Edwardian and attractive Victorian furniture is also highly regarded.

Other choices are headed by silver and jewellery, followed by art nouveau ceramics. English 'collector' porcelain, miniatures, oriental porcelain, fine carpets, lead and tin toys, golfing and other sporting memorabilia.

78    **What about oil paintings, watercolours and prints?**

The eighteenth century is a very popular investment
choice with the experts, with modern British portraits
and etchings also in demand. In paintings,
nineteenth-century artists are attractive in the £6,000
to £9,000 range, and, in watercolours, nineteenth-
century Dutch artists in the £500 to £3,000 range.

Paintings are normally the showpiece of the auction
houses and they divide their departments into several
specialist areas to cover the whole field. Phillips for
example, sub-divides its pictures department into Fine
Old Masters, Watercolours and Drawings, Fine Continental Paintings, Modern Continental Paintings, Modern British Paintings and Prints. And though paintings
require a good deal of research and cataloguing by
experts, this does not prevent a throughput of about
20,000 pictures a year in the Phillips sale room.
Sotheby's and Christie's are larger, but work in the
same way.

The best advice on buying pictures is to buy because
you like them. You will probably make money when
you sell. And if you do not you will at least have had the
pleasure of seeing the picture and won't be too put out
if it does not sell. As a general rule of thumb for
paintings, as interest rates fall and eventually go below
the rate of inflation, then the art market will boom.
People will prefer to put their money into appreciating
assets rather than gilts or other Government securities.

79    **Which precious stones are worth investing in?**

Traditionally diamonds, of good quality. For investment, it is usual to acquire a large diamond, say, in a
platinum setting. Plenty of intrinsic value, but little
craftsmanship. This investment option is, of course,
subject to the volatility of the commodity markets.

Fashion dictates which stones are popular at any time. So does purchasing ability: you buy the best you can afford. If diamonds are too expensive, people turn to others. Recently, delicately-crafted pieces, often with relatively little spent on raw materials, have been fetching increasingly good prices. Renaissance jewellery (too delicate to wear, but lovely to look at) has been fetching prices like £1,500 for a necklace of glass beads and precious stones, set in gilt.

An attribution can easily double the value of a jewel. Prices for the work of makers like Giuliano, Castellani and Falize have been high for years. Now other makers are attracting interest: a three-layer agate cameo of a bull being savaged by a lion was sold and identified as the work of a little-known nineteenth century gem engraver, William Burch. It fetched £1,800 against a pre-sale estimate of £300–£500.

Jewellery, then, is a highly active and diversified investment field.

N.B. If you decide to go into this field, acquire a 10x lens and familiarise yourself with its use so that you can study allegedly flawless stones at first hand.

---

### What period of antique jewellery is best to buy? 80

It doesn't much matter. To wear, Victorian and onwards is best. Collections are likely to be worth more than individual pieces. They also have a wider market than a flawless diamond worth a king's ransom. And, like the less expensive paintings, there is more chance that the less expensive pieces of jewellery will increase in value more quickly than the grander ones.

Naturalistic jewellery – animals, birds, flowers, trees – in perfect condition is popular at present. Regency, multi-gem jewellery sells well, although if a piece is repaired or modified, it is less valuable. Pieces are often set with sapphires, rubies and rose diamonds. Certain styles sell, notably those set with pretty stones or half pearls. 'Pretty' is the key description: that is what attracts buyers. Renaissance jewellery, when perfect, sells very well, and it is rare. Most pieces have been modified unskilfully which spoils the value and the look – you can always tell a piece that has been repaired or tampered with; try and sell it a few years after buying it, and you will be lucky to recoup your initial outlay. Cameos hold their value, if they are Renaissance ones, but are predictably rare. Roman ones, though older, are two-a-penny. Don't be misled by age.

## 81 Are furs a good investment?

The most beautiful furs have a natural life of something like twenty years. After that, the natural oils begin to dry out, and the garment begins to fall apart and look moth-eaten. Keeping it carefully in cold storage throughout the summer may increase its lifespan for a few years, but as an investment it is not a good idea to put your money into furs. There is also a strong lobby against the killing of animals for decoration. This has certainly affected some sales, and will probably continue to do so.

## 82 Are coins a worthwhile investment?

Many of the same principles apply to coins as to other alternative investments. They are a useful diversification, a long-term investment, and can make you money in the end. They too are subject to fashion, and to fluctuation in the market.

## 83 Where can I buy and sell them?

No one knows more about coins than Spink. Glendinings are the specialist London auctioneers. Christie's and Sotheby's hold auctions about every month. Join a numismatic society (lists of them can be obtained from the British Association of Numismatic Societies). Subscribe to the two main magazines, who will keep you in touch with other collectors as well as provide information about what's going on: they are *Coin Monthly* and *Coin News incorporating Coins and Medals*. Cultivate the proverbial friendly dealer, but do NOT take a rare coin to an unknown.

---

### How can the coin market be affected? 84

By obvious things like the recession, and everyone panicking and choosing to get rid of a particular sort of coin. A hoard of William I pennies discovered in 1833 immediately made the coin, previously one of the rarest, one of the most common.

The most popular coins at the moment are bullion like Krugerrands or sovereigns, or numismatic coins like British, ancient British, early Saxon or Norman, some hammered coins (those struck by hand before 1662). These are rare collectors' items, although it is important to get good advice from someone who knowns what they are talking about. It is important to go for quality rather than quantity – coins in mint condition are the ones that increase in value. At present, it is a buyer's market. There is a shortage of rare and unusual material. Two years ago the Americans entered the British market and prices soared to an unrealistic level. They are lower but more steady now, after descending rapidly, and there is little sign of change or instability.

There is a British Numismatic Trade Association, to which collectors and dealers belong, and they have an agreed code of practice. They hold an annual fair in September or October.

### 85   Do memorabilia have investment potential?

Possibly. You are in fact buying a future. Something you buy now and keep may, in some years, become more expensive and more in demand. The person who sells a collection of Dinky toys is laughing all the way to the bank. The person who bought them may not make such a profit. Good craftsmanship matters, and could sell well in some years. The price reflects the balance of supply and demand.

Many outsiders suggest that auctioneers owe their own growth (which has been very good) to inflation-induced investment interest in antiques and fine arts. But the auction houses have greatly expanded the number of categories they handle. They regularly hold sales of anything they think might interest investors. This continuing expansion has not always made them popular with the dealers. In some respects, auctioneers are the wholesalers and dealers are the retailers. Wholesale prices are much lower than retail prices, so many collectors and investors are buying direct from the auctioneers. In some fields dealers have been virtually eliminated from the market.

### 86   Are toys and trains a worthwhile investment?

Yes, provided they are in mint condition – which usually means coming in their original box – and if they are 30 or more years old. The Dinky toys, which were produced from 1933 until the closure of the factory in 1979, are regarded as the classic collectors' items. Some of the prices they fetch are staggering. A 1933 Firestone van, priced at 6d then, would now fetch £300, a Mobil gas oil tanker from the mid-1950s, £300. Rarer items include the 1955 Vulcan bomber model, worth £500.

Dinky only made 500 in 1955 and ironically they did not sell very well then!

Electric train sets are another category where prices have been particularly strong. A recent sale at Phillips (regarded as the best auction house for toys and trains), a Bassett Lowke 4-4-2 tank locomotive in near mint condition went for £1,400 against the £200–£250 expected for it. Interest is not merely confined to models. At the same sale a large collection of tickets from old railway companies, expected to make £60–£100, reached £3,200. There is a hard core of 50,000 collectors in the toy and train field, so there is plenty of scope for buying and selling. Investments will appreciate in value again as long as they are kept in mint condition.

Guidance on which toys might be good investments can be obtained from auctioneers.

---

## Do medals make good investments? 87

Yes, but like all unusual investments, it depends on which medals you choose. The really rare and most famous medals such as the Victoria Cross are, by their nature, the most valuable. Because it is the highest award for gallantry (founded by Queen Victoria in 1856 and made from the metal of guns captured at the siege of Sebastopol), only 1,348 have been issued. This has meant that the suggested minimum for a Victoria Cross has climbed from £1,500 in 1972 to around £10,000 today (though recent prices have varied from £7,500 to £110,000). The George Cross awarded for conspicuous gallantry (not in face of the enemy) is slightly less valuable. In 1972, one would fetch £600. Today, it might be £5,500.

Collectors usually start, however, with a Waterloo medal or others from the Napoleonic Wars, such as the Military General Service Medal with one of 29 bars covering different campaigns. Prices for these kinds of medals vary from £260 to £1,250 for the Fort Detroit Bar (for the American War of 1812. The table on page 115 gives an idea of how a range of medals has fared in the last ten years. Remember that inflation has pushed the cost of living up four-fold over the same period.

---

### 88 What are the points to remember?

As with all unusual investments, there are a number of points the investor should bear in mind:

1. The importance of research cannot be underestimated. It can make a big difference to the value of a medal. Whether a recipient of the Crimea Medal charged with the Light Brigade or not, for example, can make a difference of between £100 and £900 to the price of that medal.

2. NCOs' and officers' medals are more costly because there is usually more biographical detail accompanying them. A junior officer's medal can be expected to have a 40 per cent premium while a major's or above will have a 100 per cent premium.

3. Collectors like the medals to be kept in good condition and well polished (as soldiers wore them).

4. If the original naming of medals has been altered, it can have an adverse effect on the value. Renaming took place when the recipient's medal was lost or stolen and he did not wish to wear a replacement bearing someone else's name.

5. Defective medals or those that have been repaired should be avoided.

6. Re-issued or later issued medals are not as valuable.

7. Copy medals should be avoided – these will have been recently produced because of the increasing interest in medals.

# Comparison of medal prices since 1972 with estimations for 1985

| | 1972 | 1976 | 1981 | 1985 |
|---|---|---|---|---|
| | £ | £ | £ | £ |
| Victoria Cross (suggested minimum price) | 1,500 | 3,300 | 8,000 | 10,000 |
| George Cross (suggested minimum price) | 600 | 1,100 | 3,000 | 5,500 |
| Military Cross George V | 16 | 30 | 100 | 125 |
| Military Medal George V | 5 | 17 | 45 | 55 |
| Distinguished Flying Cross George VI | 42 | 80 | 220 | 275 |
| Seringapatam Medal (silver) | 40 | 110 | 200 | 250 |
| Mr. Davison's Nile Medal (bronze) | 14 | 30 | 60 | 80 |
| Mr. Moulton's Trafalgar Medal (silver) | 75 | 200 | 465 | 525 |
| Military General Service Medal bar EGYPT | 45 | 140 | 220 | 255 |
| Military General Service Medal bar FORT DETROIT | 300 | 625 | 1,000 | 1,250 |
| Naval General Service Medal bar TRAFALGAR | 120 | 550 | 875 | 900 |
| Naval General Service Medal bar SYRIA | 20 | 75 | 200 | 230 |
| Waterloo Medal (Foot Regiment) | 40 | 200 | 240 | 260 |
| Crimea Medal bar SEBASTOPOL (impressed naming) | 12 | 45 | 70 | 85 |
| 1914 Mons Star | 4 | 9 | 20 | 25 |
| Army Long Service and Good Conduct Medal (Victorian) | 4 | 9 | 40 | 50 |
| Naval Long Service and Good Conduct Medal (Victorian) | 4 | 12 | 60 | 70 |
| Coronation Medal 1911 | 4 | 6 | 15 | 20 |
| Coronation Medal 1953 | 7 | 7 | 20 | 25 |

Comparisons where possible have been taken from *The Standard Catalogue of British Orders, Decorations and Medals*, published and compiled by Spink and Son Ltd.

It is, of course, important to go to a reputable dealer because he will guarantee the medals he is selling. Price trends may be assessed from attending auctions and from dealers' lists and catalogues.

The specialists in the field are Spink. Books to read include Major Gordon's *British Battles and Medals* (Spink); Edward Joslin, *The Standard Catalogue of British Orders, Decorations and Medals* (Spink – a new edition is forthcoming).

## 89  Should I invest in firearms?

Only if you really know the business. A lot of unscrupulous people are trying to cash in on collectors' interest in the market by passing off replicas as old guns by distressing them (i.e. making the gun look much older than it actually is). Advice from experts is to buy only from reputable dealers and auction houses where fakes can be recognised and sorted out. When buying, go for the best quality and as good a condition gun as possible within your price range.

Certainly, you should not lose against inflation. Generally speaking, prices of all guns – whether old or modern sporting guns – have kept well ahead of inflation. Prices have increased by about 15 per cent a year (although they did not do so at the depth of the recession in 1980–1). Cased pairs of duelling pistols are the best buys, though a recent sale of uncased Twigg pistols (the finest of all English gunsmiths) went for £4,000, double the market estimate. But in dealing in such pistols, it is important to ensure that they have not been converted from percussion to flintlock to make them appear older.

Modern breech loading and smooth bore guns (from 1890 onwards) are often bought by sportsmen who are interested not just in an appreciating asset but in using them. In this case it is vital, of course, to keep the gun well oiled and cleaned every time it is used or rust will eat away the gun and its value. There are many established gun-makers, like Holland and Holland, or Purdey, who can provide advice on some guns, or the auctioneers will provide expert opinions.

### Are old cars a worthwhile investment? 90

Collecting old cars for investment started in a big way towards the end of the 1960s, when there was a huge boom in prices between 1969 and 1979. But the market came unstuck in 1979 and many experts have serious doubts about the 1979–89 period. So beware. The market appears to have been particularly badly hit in the middle range of collectors' cars – the £15,000 to £40,000 bracket. Soaring restoration costs (£12 an hour labour and 1,000 hours work to strip and rebuild) have hit the market, together with the cost of garaging and repairs. But experts in the field stress that it is no good buying beautiful cars just to wrap them up and leave them in a garage. They will deteriorate rapidly. Cars must be used regularly, which in turn means regular maintenance. This can cost £1,000 a year with another £500 for garaging and insurance.

But at the top end of the market, recession has little meaning for cars such as a Mercedes 500K Special Roadster, sold by Christie's in Los Angeles in 1979 for $440,000 – the highest price paid at auction for a car.

Even this price is dwarfed by the Bugatti Royale. Only eight were produced and six survive. A bid of $2.2 million was made for one recently, but it failed. At the top 10 per cent of the market, the prices have appreciated by an average of 30 per cent for 20 years. European cars are the most valuable: American cars were produced in far greater volume and in any case they are usually snapped up by American buyers.

Amongst current prices, a Bentley R Type Continental 1952 is worth £20,000, a Bugatti Type 43 Gransport 1928 £60,000, a Maserati 250F GP 1956 £100,000, a Rolls Royce Silver Ghost Alpine Eagle 1914 £65,000, and for a Mercedes Benz S Type 1928 £120,000.

Notwithstanding the risks involved (and many people thinking E type Jaguars would be good investments bought them for £6,000 to £8,000 five years ago only to find they will probably get less than half for it now) – the one area that experts believe will be worthwhile is in sports and sports racing cars.

Experts to consult include Christie's and British Car Auctions. Many cars appear at the top auction houses, who may charge 15 per cent commission. There are also a number of antique car dealers in the Kensington area of London. Be careful, because they may include a large mark-up in the car's selling price.

## 91    Should I invest in old aircraft?

Aircraft are just starting to become investment items – but there is a limited market of aircraft types. Recent World War II films have increased the demand for Spitfires and Hurricanes. They cost around £10,000 to £20,000 then, and prices have rocketed since. For example, a Spitfire has recently been sold for £260,000. Peaks were set in the sale of the Strathallen collection two years ago. A Hurricane went for £260,000 and a Spitfire fetched £140,000. Spitfires and Hurricanes – because they are very well known – are regarded as the best investments. In the USA, the P51 Mustang and other World War II high performance fighters are similarly collectors' items (bigger bomber aircraft are not regarded as investments).

But there are drawbacks. The aircraft – like cars –

need to be flown regularly to prevent deterioration. Running costs can be £800 to £1,000 per hour. Much of this goes on fuel (60-plus gallons an hour at £2.20 a gallon) and insurance premiums. Storage costs and the strict maintenance required by the Civil Aviation Authority (CAA) push costs higher still. The very stringent CAA rules do, however, make this sort of flying very safe indeed.

At the other end of the scale, fabric and wood biplanes of the pre- and early-World War II era have good potential for the future. Tiger Moths stand out here. Four years ago they cost £9,000 to £10,000. Today that figure is £17,000 to £19,000 and they will continue to improve. Older biplanes of World War I vintage are not regarded as good investments because they are too difficult to fly, are very unstable and much too dependent on the weather.

To find out more about the aircraft market, contact the large auctioneers.

## Is wine worth buying for investment? 92

Yes, on the whole, subject to luck and market fluctuation. However, the most important attribute for collecting and investing in wine is to like it, because, if the very worst comes to the worst, you can still enjoy drinking it.

Historically the best wines for investment have been claret and vintage port. Claret has always produced a more spectacular rate of return; vintage port takes longer. Stick to first growths in clarets and perhaps some second and third growth. This will cost from about £350 a case. The market crashed in 1973–4, but since 1975 it has been steadily improving. There are no signs of this changing. For example, Chateau Latour 1975 claret which has always had a good reputation was available for £150 a case in 1976, and now fetches £500 a case at auction. This is doing very well indeed, giving something like 20 per cent compound interest. You are more likely to achieve 15 per cent. Vintage port has been doing well recently.

When you buy, it is always best to get in early, when the annual growths are first offered. It will be about two years before they will be ready for shipping. There should be no problems about delay if you go to a well-constituted company, though there have been and still unfortunately are cases of even well-known companies becoming insolvent, in which case it is unlikely that you will ever see your wine, although you have paid for it in advance.

## 93 Do I need to know about wine before I start and where can I find out about it?

Yes. This increases your enjoyment, and is also sensible. The Sunday Telegraph's *Good Wine Guide* is a good place to start. Hugh Johnson is prolific, and has produced several books. Michael Broadbent is Sotheby's resident wine expert, and has written *The Great Vintage Wine Book*. Other useful books include Jancis Robinson's *The Great Wine Book*, and Clive Coates's *Claret*. Advice is freely available from the auction houses and from reputable dealers.

## 94 Can I invest for other people?

Yes. You can establish a trust under Deed of Covenant thus achieving significant tax savings as well as laying down good wine for the future. The covenant is between the donor and the child (one generation removed). The child's parent or guardian is the trustee,

and wines will always be chosen and invoiced to the
trustee. It is possible for the investor to deduct income
tax at the basic rate and for the parent and trustee to
reclaim the tax on behalf of the child and add this to the
investment, turning, say, £700 into £1,000. The maximum amount on which tax may be reclaimed is the
child's income allowance and any income which the
child is already receiving must be deducted from this.

Some wine merchants run investment plans offering
differently priced selections of various wines for drinking in the future. The ones with the finest wines should
show a healthy capital appreciation in the future, after
about five or six years in reserve. The wines are bought
young and kept. There is no point in buying good wine
unless it is stored well. You can store wine either in a
cellar or, if you don't have one, at a wine merchants.
Contact a wine merchant for details.

### Is it possible to share out the cost?                    95

Forming a buying syndicate has benefits in terms of the
discounts some merchants will offer for purchases of
three or five cases, or ten or more. Be certain to sort out
in advance who gets what, and if the wine is kept in the
same cellar, issue duplicate records. You should keep
records, in any case, of what wine you buy and sell. In
the last war records of ownership were lost, and there
are stocks of wonderful wine improving wonderfully in
cellars all over the country with no one to say who owns
them.

### Should I collect stamps?                                 96

Stamps are heading out of the recession, according to
stamp auction realisations and retail sales figures.

There was an initial drop in values in 1980, but since then stamps have weathered the problems of the recession quite well and are re-gaining the ground that they lost. The independent survey, 'Stamp Price Movements 1960–1983' compiled by the P & E Consulting Group, shows that even in the period 1980–3 stamps overall had a growth rate of 10 per cent per annum. The Consumers' Association's book, *Saving and Investing* (1982), showed stamps to be one of the most lucrative of the alternative investment areas.

There is a difference in approach to investing in and to collecting stamps. In other alternative investment areas, you are encouraged to make a collection in order to increase the value of your investment. But while to collect a whole country's stamps, for example, from the first to the most recent, would indeed make a valuable investment (depending on the country) it would be very expensive and time-consuming. Thus stamp 'collectors' are those interested in philately, while 'investors' often do not progress to becoming collectors. Advice is vital, and available from a company like the well-known Stanley Gibbons, or from an auction house's resident expert.

Currently, Commonwealth stamps are popular. Other countries have their vogues – the instance, Rhodesia when it became independent, and the Falklands, more recently. Many of the higher-priced 'classic' items suitable for investment have now fallen and stabilised at their 1979 price levels, so it is a very good time to buy. All the recent auctions show that collectors are now buying these again, and are often paying more than the auctioneers' estimates. Ten years ago, the 1840 Penny Black, in top condition, would have sold for £20. At the peak of the market in 1979–80, the stamp would have sold for £300 and at the market's low in summer 1982 its value had fallen to £150. Recently, one sold at auction for £250. Stamps are a medium- to long-term investment – up to ten years. In any given ten-year period stamps have always kept well ahead of inflation and offered attractive rates of return.

Stamp collecting should be thought of as a diversification; it would be foolish to put all your money into stamps, but for an investment of anything from £100 upwards, you can expect a reasonable return over ten years or so. When the market stabilises again, investors may be able to return to a holding period of five years. For safe investing, Stanley Gibbons recommend only classic items of up to 1900 and certain items up to 1930 in very fine condition. Investors can, of course, make good profits on selective middle issues and more modern stamps, but this is more speculative.

An investor with Gibbons can choose either to place an initial sum with the company and add further amounts at regular intervals, and so build up an investment collection, or to buy an investment portfolio with a once-only lump sum. There is no charge for the service. Gibbons will either store and insure the stamps for you, at a small charge, on a rising scale, or you can keep them in a bank. It is important to take care with the storage conditions – keep stamps flat and cool, at a steady temperature.

## 'D'ya wanna buy a horse?' 97

You can make money by investing in bloodstock, but it's rather like investing in a lottery with extremely expensive tickets. The question to ask is, can I justify the cost of the investment with the pleasure I will derive from owning and racing a horse? There are ways of minimising the expenditure. There are no guarantees, though. Some say that if you buy horses as foals and sell them as yearlings again the following autumn you should not lose; your own risk is lessened because you do not race the horse but leave that to someone else. (A yearling is a one-year-old needing training for its race debut over six furlongs as a two-year-old.) About 4,500 thoroughbred foals are born in this country every year. There are just over half that number of two year olds on the racecourse. The season for flat racing runs from the third week in March to the second week in November. The National Hunt season (jump racing) is from August to May. In terms of investment, flat racing is more lucrative. National Hunt prize money is often low, while flat racing has higher prizes, though it is more expensive and is not for the lone amateur enthusiast.

## 98    How do I buy a thoroughbred

Enlist the aid of a reputable agency like to British Bloodstock Agency, which is based in London and Newmarket. The agency will advise on all bloodstock matters from purchasing and insurance to registration and syndication. They charge a commission of between 5 and 10 per cent, depending on the costs incurred in retaining the horse. Yearlings are bought from four main sales: Doncaster after the St Leger, Goffs sale in Ireland in September, the Newmarket sales in September, and the Houghton yearling sales in October, again at Newmarket. All thoroughbred horses have January 1st of the year of their birth as their birthday. (The gestation period is eleven months and the covering season is from 15 February to 30 June, so two yearlings could differ in age by as much as six months.) Get advice when you buy, and be cautious about buying an unraced two-year-old.

## What about tax? 99

Since only a very small percentage of horses in training
will win enough to cover training costs, if you own the
horse as a private individual, you can legitimately claim
to be following a hobby. Winnings are free of tax and a
horse is a tangible, moveable asset with an expectancy
of life of less than 50 years, and therefore not eligible for
CGT. As long as the horse is not used for breeding, it
should not, in itself, attract VAT, other than in the
initial purchase and subsequent sale.

## Can I save on a horse's running costs? 100

You can buy the horse through a limited company.
Remember that the Jockey Club will need to register
the name of the horse (which would refer to the company).

It costs something like £5,000 a year to keep a horse
in training. Insurance and veterinary fees are an extra
£1,000 a year. A good horse, after its three-year-old
career, is retired to stud. There should then be a huge
demand for this stallion as a sire, and astronomical
sums have been paid for syndicate shares in such an
animal. During the covering season, a healthy stallion
should cover 40 mares, requiring about 110–20 cover-
ings. The stallion is divided into 40 shares, giving each
shareholder the right to send a mare each year to the
stallion, or sell his nomination to another mare owner.
Each shareholder contributes to the cost of keeping the
stallion. If mating is successful, the foal will be born 11
months later. A year later, the horse is sold at a price
reflecting is parentage. After another year the horse
will run and show whether it has inherited the fast
genes of its sire.

If you have bought a filly, the case is rather different. There is no need to take the horse out of training after three-year-old success. She would run as a four-year-old and possibly increase her winnings. When released from training, a filly will require a nomination. This should be considered cautiously. If the match is a successful one, it will still be five years before the initial mating can be judged to be financially successful. N.B. Total running costs for all the horses on the flat are about five or six times total prize money.

There are several City schemes for private investors to buy a share in a racing or breeding company. Ask your broker or professional adviser for details of these.

# X
# Useful addresses

## I Introduction

The Law Society
113 Chancery Lane
London WC2 (01-242 1222)

Inland Revenue
Somerset House
Strand
London WC2 (01-438 6622)

## 2 Saving your money

British Insurance Association
Aldermary House
Queen Street
London EC4 (01-248 4477)

Barclays Bank

Life Offices Association
Aldermary House
Queen Street
London EC4 (01-248 4477)
54 Lombard Street
London EC3 (01-623 4311)

Trustee Savings Bank
3 Copthall Avenue
London EC2 (01-588 9292)

Building Societies Association
14 Park Street
London W1 (01-629 0515)

Co-operative Bank
78 Cornhill
London EC3 (01-283 5691)

Lloyds Bank
71 Lombard Street
London EC3 (01-626 1500)

Midland Bank
Poultry
London EC2 (01-606 9911)

National Giro Bank
10 Milk Street
London EC2 (01-600 6020)

National Westminster Bank
41 Lothbury
London EC2 (01-606 6060)

Williams and Glyns
20 Birchin Lane
London EC2 (01-623 4356)

Royal Bank of Scotland
42 St Andrews Square
Edinburgh EH2 2YE
(031 596 8555)

Clydesdale Bank
30 St Vincent Place
Glasgow G1 2HL
(041 248 7070)

Bank of Scotland
The Mound
Edinburgh RH1 1YZ
(031 221 7071)

### 3 National Savings

Department for National
Savings
375 Kensington High Street
London W14 (01-603 2000)

Department for National
Savings
Bonds and Stock Office
Preston New Road
Marten, Blackpool
Lancashire FY3 91P
(0253 66151)

### 4 Stocks and shares

The Stock Exchange
London EC2 (01-588 2355)

Unit Trust Association
Park House
Finsbury Circus
London EC2 (01-628 0871)

### 5 Other financial markets

London Commodity Exchange
Cereal House
Mark Lane
London EC3 (01-481 2080)

London Metal Exchange
Plantation House
Fenchurch Street
London EC3 (01-626 3311)

Lloyds of London
Lime Street
London EC3 (01-623 7100)

LIFFE
Royal Exchange
London EC3 (01-623 0444))

International Gold Corporation
30 St George Street
London W1 (01-499 9201)

De Beers Consolidated Mines
Ltd
40 Holborn Viaduct
London EC1 (01-353 1577)

### 6 Property

British Property Timeshare
Association
Langham House
308 Regent Street
London W1 (01-637 8049)

National House Building
Council
58 Portland Place
London W1 (01-637 1248)

Royal Institute of Chartered
Surveyors
12 Great George Street
London SW1 (01-222 7000)

Department of the
Environment
2 Marsham Street
London SW1 (01-212 4688)

Incorporated Society of Valuers
and Auctioneers
9 Cadogan Gate
London SW1 (01-235 2282)

National Association of Estate
Agents
Arbon House
21 Jury Street
Warwick CV34 4EH (0926
496800)

### Forestry

Economic Forestry Group
Forestry House
Great Haseley
Oxford OX9 7PG (08446 571)

Fountain Forestry
37 Queen Anne Street
London W1M 9FB
(01-631 0485)

### Farming

Strutt & Parker
13 Hill Street
London W1X 8DL
(01-629 7282)

Smiths Gore
Fielden House
Little College Street
London SW1P 3SH
(01-222 4054)

**Funds for small investors
include:**
Property Growth Assurance
Keon House
High Street
Croydon CR9 1LU
(01-680 0606)

City of Westminster Assurance
Sentry House
500 Avebury Boulevard
Saxon Gate West
Milton Keynes MK9 2LA
(0908 606101)

University Medical General
St Brandon's House
29 Great George Street
Bristol BS1 5QT
(0272 276954/211988)

Agricultural Land Share
Investments Ltd
1 Brewer's Green
Buckingham Gate
London SW1H 0RB
(01-222 5331)

**7 Small Businesses**
*Small Firms Information Centres:*

The national Freefone number
is 2444

*Scotland*
57 Bothwell Street
Glasgow G2 6TU
(041 248 6014)

*Wales*
16 St David's House
Wood Street
Cardiff CF1 1ER (0222 396116)

*North*
3 Cloth Market
Central House
Newcastle upon Tyne
NE1 1EU
(0632 325353)

*North West*
320-325 Royal Exchange
Building
St Anne's Square
Manchester M2 7AH (061 832
5282)

*Yorkshire and Humberside*
1 Park Row
City Square
Leeds LS1 5NR (0532 445151)

*East Midlands*
48-50 Maid Marian Way
Nottingham NG1 6GF
(0602 49791)

*West Midlands*
6th Floor Ladywood House
Stephenson Street
Birmingham B2 4DT
(021 643 3344)

*East*
24 Brooklands Avenue
Cambridge CB2 2BU
(0223 63312)

*London and South East*
123 Victoria Street
London SW1 (01-212 5492)

*South West*
Colston Centre
Colston Avenue
Bristol BS1 4UB (0272 294546)

A similar service is provided in
Northern Ireland by the
Department of Commerce.

*The Scottish Council (Development and Industry)*
1 Castle Street, Edinburgh EH2 3AJ. They also have offices in
Glasgow, Aberdeen, Inverness and London. Their aim is to
promote the industrial and social development of Scotland.

*Enterprise North*
This is a voluntary organisation working through New Enterprise
Panels in seven areas in the North East and Cumbria, and is made
up of businessmen with years of experience in the financial,
technical and marketing fields, whose sole aim is to help establish
successful business ventures in the north. The Co-ordinating
Centre, Enterprise North, Durham University Business School,
Mill Hill Lane, Durham CH1 3LB (0385 41919, ext 42).

*The National Research and Development Corporation*
Details from the Commercial Services Controller, Industrial
Development Office, National Research and Development Office,
Kingsgate House, 66–74 Victoria Street, London SW1 6SL (01-828
3400).

*Department of Industry*
The Department can give Regional Development Grants to what
they call "assisted areas". These are divided into three categories:
intermediate areas, development areas and special development
areas, and the scale of the grant varies according to which type of
area you qualify for. Most assisted areas are in the North and North
West of Britain including Wales and Scotland. Write for
information to the Regional Development Grants Division,
Department of Industry, Millbank, London SW1.

*Local Enterprise Trust*
The Trust is defined as "a broadly-based local group involved in the
creation of worthwhile work through the fostering and development
of small scale enterprises". Further information from the
Association of Local Enterprise Trusts, Wilton Corner, 10 Grenfell
Road, Beaconsfield, Buckinghamshire (04946 3080).

*Crafts Advisory Committee*
12 Waterloo Place, London SW1Y 4AU (01-839 6306).

*National Federation of the Self Employed*
32 St Annes Road West, Lytham St Annes, Lancashire (0253
720911). This represents over 50,000 self-employed and small
business people. They campaign against 'discriminatory and
pernicious legislation, penal and confiscatory taxation, imposed
without regard for justice and the basic right of freedom'.

*The Forum of Private Business Limited*
Ruskin Rooms, Drury Lane, Knutsford, Cheshire WA16 0ED
(0565 4467/8). Their aim is to get a greater voice for private and
professional people in the legislation which affects them.

Investors in Industry
91 Waterloo Road
London SE1 (01-928 7822)

London Enterprise Agency
69 Cannon Street
London EC4 (01-236 2676)

## Art, antiques and others

British Antique Dealers'
Association
20 Rutland Gate
London SW7 1BD
(01-589 4128)

The London and Provincial
Antique Dealers' Association
112 Brompton Road
London SW3 (01-584 0294)

Phillips
7 Blenheim Street,
London W1 (01-629 6602)

Christie's
South Kensington
85 Old Brompton Road
London SW7 (01-581 2231)

Christie's
South Kensington
85 Old Brompton Road
London SW7 (01-581 2231)

Bonham's
Montpelier Street
London SW7 (01-584 9161)

Sotheby's
34 New Bond Street
London W1 (01-493 8080)

**Coins**
British Numismatic Trade
Association
(Secretary, Mrs C. Deane)
P.O. Box 52C
Esher
Surrey KT10 8PW
(0372 62568)

British Association of
Numismatic Societies
(Hon. Sec. K.F. Sugden)
Department of Numismatics
Manchester Museum
The University
Oxford Road
Manchester

Seaby's Coins and Medals
16 Charing Cross Road
London WC2 (01-836 0631)

Spink & Son Ltd
King Street
London SW1 (01-930 7888)

**Dealers**
A H Baldwin & Sons Ltd
11 Adelphi Terrace
London WC2 (01-930 6879)

Stanley Gibbons Currency Ltd
395 Strand
London WC2 (01-836 8444)

Lubbocks
315 Regent Street
London W1 (01-637 7922)

**Cars**
British Car Auctions
Expedier House
Union Road
Farnham
Surrey (0252 711222)

**Wine**

Wine and Spirit Educational
Trust
5 King's House
Kennet Wharf Lane
Upper Thames Street
London EC4V 3AJ
(01-236 3551/2)

*Leading merchants include:*
Justerini & Brooks
61 St James's Street
London SW1A 1LZ
(01-493 8721)
and
39 George Street
Edinburgh EG2 2HN
(01-226 4202)

Berry Bros & Rudd Ltd
3 St James's Street
London SW1 (01-930 1888)

Saccone & Speed Ltd
11 Cosmo Place
London WC1 (01-837 6578)

**Stamps**

Stanley Gibbons Ltd
399 Strand
London WC2R 0LX
(01-836 8444)

**Racing**

The British Bloodstock Agency
Ltd
11a Albemarle Street
London W1 (01-493 9402)

Racehorse Owners' Association
42 Portman Square
London W1 (01-486 6977)

# A word or two about offshore funds.

# Hill Samuel.

Making the right choice from the many offshore funds available can be difficult. However, there is an answer which doesn't mean limiting your potential. Choose Hill Samuel.

We offer a comprehensive range of funds investing in the world's major investment areas and stock markets.

Far East, High Technology, U.S. Equities, U.K. Equities, Gilts, Bonds and Currency Funds are available. They have achieved consistently good results and may all be linked to a Flexible Savings Plan.

The funds are managed by Hill Samuel Investment Management International, the overseas arm of Hill Samuel Group which already has total investments of over £4,500,000,000 under advice and management.

Funds are managed through offices in Jersey, Channel Islands or through Bank von Ernst & Cie. AG, a wholly-owned Hill Samuel subsidiary in Berne, Switzerland.

If you'd like to know more about our funds contact D. H. Humpleby, Hill Samuel (Channel Islands) Trust Company Limited, 7 Bond Street, St. Helier, Jersey, Channel Islands. Tel: 0534 73244. Telex: 4192167.

# HILL SAMUEL INVESTMENT MANAGEMENT INTERNATIONAL
JERSEY                                                                    SWITZERLAND

## A range of business and personal finance books from Telegraph Publications

### A Consumer's Guide to Buying and Selling a Home
**A Family Money-Go-Round Special**
**by Diana Wright**
Covers all aspects of buying and selling a home, including the various types of mortgage available, which one to choose, how to get a mortgage, the costs of moving and the problems posed by financial circumstances. Essential reading for the first-time buyer or anyone thinking of moving house.
**£3.95. Available May 1985.**

### A Consumer's Guide to Air Travel
**A Family Money-Go-Round Special**
**by Frank Barrett**
The popular, value-for-money guide to the variety of cheap air fares on offer. Shows you how to choose your travel agent, with details on bucket shops, pre-flight checks, passengers' rights and corporate travel.
**£3.95**

### A Consumer's Guide to Lump-Sum Investment
**A Family Money-Go-Round Special**
**by Diana Wright**
A comprehensive guide telling you what sort of returns you should expect from your investment, the importance of tax regulations, what you can invest your money in and where to go for professional advice. An invaluable guide to the whole range of lump-sum investments from bonds to securities.
**£3.95. Available July 1985.**

### A Consumer's Guide to Leaving Money to Children
### A Family Money-Go-Round Special
### by John Turner

An invaluable guide, illuminating the complex subject of Capital Transfer Tax and discussing the ways in which assets can be passed on to children with maximum benefit. Gives details of the possibilities offered by deeds of covenant, gifts, businesses, shares, reversions, options and trusts.
£3.95

### How to Set Up and Run Your Own Business
### A Daily Telegraph Business Enterprise Handbook

An essential guide for those setting up or running a small business, with contributions from leading professionals in the fields of commerce and finance.
£4.95 p/b £7.95 h/b. Available May 1985.

### Building Your Business Series:

### How to Win Profitable Business
### by Tom Cannon

Concentrates on practical ideas and methods, which, turned into action, result in full order books, a busy factory and work force, and increased growth, turnover and profits.
£5.95 p/b £9.95 h/b

### How to Manage Money
### by G.D. Donleavy and M. Metcalfe

A lucid and comprehensive guide on how to make your money work harder for you in business. Knowing where your money lies and how to control it leads to better financial planning and costs control, sound budgets and an insight into your accounts which leads to better business decisions.
£5.95 p/b £9.95 h/b

**How to Manage People**
**by Ron Johnson**
Contains everything you need to know about
motivating staff, getting the very best out of them and
keeping them keen, efficient and happy.
**£5.95 p/b £9.95 h/b**

**Know Your Law**
**by Greville Janner**
Provides all the practical answers to legal problems
your business is likely to meet.
**£5.95p/b £9.95h/b**